PRAISE FOR HEALI[N…]
OTHER S[…]

'It is important with a work like this to steer clear of the flaky and the 'pop' so as not to be dismissed as such. *Healing from the Other Side* is a very comprehensive book that clearly lays out the procedures for practicing past life regression, giving good examples to show exactly how it works. It is a really interesting read, and would hold the imagination of anybody interested in the subject of past lives, giving many hints and tips as to how to explore them effectively. I think that anyone who reads it will feel well equipped to actually start doing past life therapy themselves in a safe and structured way.'

– ***Dr John Rowan***, *Psychologist and Author of*
The Transpersonal, Subpersonalities,
The Reality Game and Ordinary Ecstasy.
Fellow of the United Kingdom Council for Psychotherapy, the British Psychological Society and the British Association for Counselling and Psychotherapy

'I feel both happy and honoured that Dr Tom Barber and Dr Sandra Westland asked me to read and comment on their book *Healing from the Other Side*. Why? Because it is pragmatic, clear, positive, grounded with references, well-written, expressive, with a clear motivational tone and good examples. Why pragmatic? Because it goes straight to the point and it has very constructive and useful exercises. Why positive? Because it points towards ways not just to 'fix' past-life troubles but also to give ongoing ones a boost in clarity and happiness. Aside from this, the theory is there, with an obvious capacity for synthetizing relevant knowledge both from neurology and psychology, placing in perspective the way modified states of consciousness become a big part of the hypnotic game, both at the service of therapists and their clients. I especially enjoyed their presentation of concepts such as closing past loops and even ongoing ones. I have been around as a therapist and I can assert that through examples, techniques and the way they outline sessions Tom and Sandra are showing hypnotic art at its best, and their book is showing therapeutic intent with a literary smile to us all.'

*– **Dr Vitor Rodrigues**, Psychologist, Psychotherapist and Author of Terras de Mentes.*
Past President of the European Transpersonal Association and the Luso-Brazilian Transpersonal Association

'*Healing from the Other Side* is an extraordinary book. Dr Tom Barber and Dr Sandra Westland have taken great care to present a very clear, complete, and detailed piece of work. They elaborate on many of the facets of past life regression therapy that are of great importance, including some of the approaches I work with myself in Transgenerational Psychotherapy and Ontogonia. This book will take you deeper into your own existence in a profound and loving way, and is a wonderfully interesting and important addition to the literature that I have become completely immersed in. Thank you!'

*– **Professor María Guadalupe Medina Gallardo**, PhD, Clinical and Medical Hypnotherapist,*
Founder of the Instituto de Psicoterapia Humanista (IDEPH)

'*Healing from the Other Side* is a fantastic book on past life regression therapy that will have a broad appeal. It encourages the reader to open up their creative mind to all possibilities for healing and clearing. The chapters are bursting with tips and techniques for exploring the unconscious mind and developing a greater sense of self-awareness. It is written in an uplifting style that is both easy and engaging and shows us why past life regression therapy can be such an effective healing process. Many books written about past life regression tend to preach to the converted, but this book will appeal to a wide audience and maybe even a few sceptics. It is also an excellent manual for any therapist who wants to incorporate past life regression therapy into their practice. I fully recommend this wonderful, vibrant book for anyone looking to deepen their self-awareness and heal blocks, both physical and energetic. On top of that it may just open a door of discovery into one or more of your own past lives!'

– ***Glenn Harrold***, *Clinical Hypnotherapist, Composer and Bestselling Author of The Answer. Fellow of The British School of Clinical Hypnosis*

'Are you interested in expanding your mind? If you are ready for a uniquely interesting and thought-provoking book, consider *Healing from the Other Side* by Dr Tom Barber and Dr Sandra Westland. While many books are available regarding spiritual approaches to hypnosis and past lives, very few seem to be credibly researched and written with appropriate references as this comprehensive book is. It is further enhanced with some meditation and hypnosis exercises as well as the authors own professional experience with clients.'

– ***Roy Hunter***, *DIMDHA, DAPHP; Hypnosis Trainer and Published Author of The Art of Spiritual Hypnosis, The Art of Hypnosis and Hypnosis for Inner Conflict Resolution*

Healing From The Other Side

HEALING FROM THE OTHER SIDE

The Guide to Breaking Down Barriers
and Finding Freedom Through
Past Life Regression Therapy

Dr Tom Barber and Dr Sandra Westland

CCTS PUBLICATIONS
LONDON

Healing from the Other Side: The Guide to Breaking Down Barriers and Finding Freedom through Past Life Regression Therapy.
By Dr Tom Barber and Dr Sandra Westland.

First published in 2018 by CCTS Publications.
Contemporary College of Therapeutic Studies Ltd.
Kemp House, 152 City Road, London, EC1V 2NX, UK
www.cctspublications.com

All enquiries should be addressed to CCTS Publications at books@cctspublications.com.

British Library Cataloguing Publication Data
A catalogue record for this book is available from the British Library

ISBN: 978-0-9926804-3-5

First Edition, published in 2018 by CCTS Publications, an imprint of Contemporary College of Therapeutic Studies Ltd.

Other Books by the Authors

Thinking Therapeutically

By Dr Tom Barber and Dr Sandra Westland

The Midas Touch

With Dr Tom Barber and Dr Sandra Westland

Smashing Your Glass Ceiling

By Dr Sandra Westland

The Book on Back Pain

By Dr Tom Barber

ACKNOWLEDGMENTS

We would like to thank all those students that have pushed themselves out of their comfort zone to experience Past Life Transpersonal Therapy in our courses, as well as those that delved into their own past lives in personal therapy with us, whether by choice or by surprise. Without you this book would not have been possible. This especially goes out to clients that we have presented in this book: Prea, Idai, Agnes, and Maarja.

Our thanks go out to Rosalie Williams for her continued support in always pointing us in the right direction for the help we need. Because of Rosalie's kindness we were fortunate to have crossed paths with our excellent editor, Peter Young. Peter has brought so much to this book, and we owe him a great deal of gratitude for his first-class professionalism. Our co-editor, Darcy Werkman, has also elevated the book tremendously, for which we are very grateful. Thanks also go to Siva, for his excellent work in the book design.

Further thanks go to one of the most profoundly inspirational figures in the transpersonal world, Dr John Rowan. To have received John's guidance in our writing was a privilege and honour. The same appreciation is given to our esteemed colleague and friend, Dr Vitor Rodrigues, a vibrant shining light in the world of human consciousness. Additionally, not to mention the role of Professor Jure Biechonski in the continued development of our ideas would be omitting a major influence on our work. Thanks Jure, our dear friend.

In writing about past lives we have studied the work of many of the leading authors and practitioners in the field, some now passed to the next part of their eternal journey through time, and some still here in preparation. Whilst there is a long list of authors whose work has been of tremendous help to us in formulating this book, most notable among these, to whom we owe a debt of gratitude, are Dr Roger Woolger, Dr Brain Weiss, Andy Tomlinson, Dr Michael Newton, Carol Bowman, Dr Ian Stevenson, and Tom Schroder.

In writing a book like this it is inevitable you cross paths with those that have forged the way for learning and insight. We were lucky enough in this sense to have gained valuable feedback from Glenn Harrold, helping us on our journey to declaring *Healing from the Other Side* a book worthy of writing. Our sincere thanks also go to both Professor María Guadalupe Medina Gallardo, and Roy Hunter, who gave up their valuable time to review the book in its rawest format.

Finally, we hope this book demonstrates that we are all on a journey. We are encountering life exactly as we were destined to. Nothing is out of place, and everything is part of our life's design, just as it was intended.

Contents

~ PART TWO ~

Introduction
A Good Beginning Makes a Good Ending

The real voyage of discovery consists not in seeking new landscapes, but in having new eyes.
Marcel Proust

The Transpersonal Bar

Two existential psychotherapists, meeting at the end of a conference on the nature of freedom, choice, and responsibility, walk into a transpersonal psychology bar. One of them asks the barman, "Can I get the meaning to life here?" The barman replies, "Sure, which life would you like meaning to?" The other therapist, feeling curiously hopeful at what else might be on offer, asks, "Well . . . can I get some purpose also?" to which the barman replies, "Sure, the higher one? No problem. Two of them coming up!"

The therapists look at each other, confused at this somewhat cheerful and positive attitude, and say to the barman, "So, you mean to say that when people come into your bar they can order 'meaning' and 'purpose', just like that, no questions asked!?" The barman replies, "For sure! We serve many things in my truly transpersonal bar, but the people that come in here only ever get what they seek." One of the existentialists nudges their colleague's arm, goading them to ask the blindingly obvious therapeutic question, "But what if they don't know what they want?" The barman responds, "Then, my friends, they will always certainly get what they are given." The other existentialist asks, bursting to know, "But what will that be?" The transpersonal barman replies, "Well, of course . . . they'll receive exactly what they need."

And so our ever-evolving journey of discovery into the limitless dimensions of what it is to be human continued.

In the Beginning

We've been here before, you and us. We don't know when, where, or how. But once upon a time for some reason we existed in each other's lives in some shape or form. The question arises: why are we here together again, right here, right now, and for what reasons?

You may never have considered that the people you know, meet, and have come into contact with, either personally or through a book like this, have likely at some point in history been a part of your life. But as we begin this journey, consider what it would be like to open your mind to this concept, because in doing so you will be able to connect to where you will find your answers, and a whole new world of discovery can open up for you.

We all have something to learn from our time together: something to heal, something to let go of, something to say, or some unfinished business to close. We also have some potential to realise, some direction and meaning to discern, and the chance to be our most authentic self, feeling fully alive and connected to others. All of this you will work out once you enter this journey from your other, less rational side, as we guide you through this book.

So let's go back to the beginning. We've been here before. Maybe one of us (Tom or Sandra) was your brother or sister, one of your parents, or one of your children. Perhaps a teacher, a lover, or friend. Or perhaps we were there to guide you when you needed it most. Maybe we were people who simply showed you kindness in your darkest hours. One of us could have even been someone who challenged you, or got under your skin and who made you angry –

but you never said. Who knows? Well, actually, you do and we do. Deep within us we know who we were to each other and we know why we are here together again as we take the first steps on this enlightening journey.

The Sole Meaning of Life – Discovering Your Purpose through Past Lives

We're sure at some point over the years that have led you up to today that you have questioned your life, asking yourself what you're doing and where your life is heading. Some people, when they ask big questions, come to the conclusion that "there must be more than this". They ponder on the idea that there must be some greater plan or meaning or purpose in life, but they're just not sure what that is. It's common – and actually healthy – to question life, *your* life and the 'hows' and 'whys' of it all. There is also an understandable concern and curiosity around what happens after your body decides to stop and the finality of your current form presents itself.

Because these questions are fundamental to life and can be difficult to find answers for, if you can't settle them with some sort of idea, they never quite go away. If you have no answers to consider, you may well form some kind of distraction to keep those questions from creeping into your thoughts and worrying you. The busyness of life and the everyday things that need your attention – work, family, paying the bills, planning the next holiday, making sure homework is completed, and checking the water boiler is serviced and the dog is walked – are all very plausible distractions. They keep you from asking those big life questions that would focus you on the bigger picture of meaning and purpose such as, "What am I doing? Is this it? And what more can I do with my life?" and so on.

However, problems can arise if you don't at some point step back and examine your life, to see if you are content with how it looks. Symptoms of living in a misaligned manner can slowly and subtly creep up on you. Often anxiety is experienced as a calling for you to attend to the deeper issues that are troubling you, niggling away under the surface or swamped out by everyday living. Depression can wrap itself around you if you are unconsciously ignoring your desire for more in life and have instead settled for less. Addictions can take over and control you, coaxing you with a false sense of hope that this is a way of helping you manage and control the mundane. If you don't attend to yourself, if you keep thinking that there is nothing more than what is in your conscious mind and what you are experiencing around you – just buildings, things, nature, people, and so on – you can eventually feel restricted. You become stuck and constrained by logic and nothing more.

If you don't connect with your meaning, purpose and essential nature, you may find that you are missing out on a whole new level of experiencing life. Somewhere within you'll know this. You will feel it. And the only way to catch your attention is for life to provide you with symptoms. Past life therapy can help you find greater understanding and resolution to these problematic symptoms and it most certainly helps with the expansion of your mind. It can open you up to finding your life's meaning and purpose, and bring you a greater sense of aliveness.

What You Can Achieve through Past Life Transpersonal Therapy

Through the process of healing with this approach, you can:

- Find out how your present life is being influenced by your past.
- Relieve symptoms and heal unwanted physical, emotional, spiritual, financial, and relationship challenges.
- Break through patterns and blocks in your life.
- Find and energise your natural talents and abilities.
- Expand your intuition and be able to tune into intuitive messages.
- Awaken the spiritual, creative aspects of you to establish a more harmonious approach to life.

- Experience a deeper connection to yourself, the world, and other people.
- Innovate an exciting future.
- Find and feel your true purpose and live a more consciously aware and aligned life.

How to Make the Most of this Book

Fundamentally, this book will teach you our view of the underlying theory and process of Past Life Transpersonal Therapy (or as we often refer to it, PLTT). If you are reading this book in the hope that you can learn how past life therapy can help you personally, then you will gain a detailed background knowledge of the process. It includes guided visualisations through the past life experience, as well as detailing how the method has helped others just like you, through a well-versed step-by-step process. If you practice as a psychotherapist, hypnotherapist, counsellor, or healer drawn to PLTT, you may be wanting to add a different perspective to helping your clients, or delve further into working with the creative imagination, and soulful expression. This book will also give you such a method. Whichever way you have found us, we recommend you relate to the book with a sense of curiosity about your own past lives and those of others.

We will teach you here how to sharpen the focus of your attention and gain greater self-connection and engagement with your intuition. You'll learn how to go beyond the traditional dimensions of the physical known world, lower your brain waves, and enter the deeper realms of an altered state of awareness and level of consciousness. This is where you will find your answers, your release and your healing.

Chapters Unfolding

The book is divided into two parts. Part 1, which encompasses Chapters 1 to 6, focusses on the theoretical underpinnings of Past Life Transpersonal Therapy. It goes into depth about the various ideas and notions that the method draws on and which are important to have explored prior to using PLTT. It looks also to get you considering your own life, and aspects of your personal growth and development. We hope it opens you to a greater connection with yourself.

Part 2, Chapters 7 through to 12, focuses on the therapeutic application of PLTT, moving into visualisations and case studies. As we move through this part of the book we slowly break the entire process down step by step, with examples from real verified client sessions. The video recordings of these sessions are available at www.healingfromtheotherside.com.

In Chapter 1 that follows we share with you our journey from the notion of symptom relief, to exploring the existential undercurrents that fundamentally flavour the experience of living. From there we venture into the nature of the transpersonal world, and how the concepts within it inspire a greater connection with life, and the journey into becoming more. We present a real-life example that demonstrates the life-changing benefits of Past Life Transpersonal Therapy.

In Chapter 2 we look at how important having an 'active imagination' is in healing the brain, mind, body, and soul, as well as introducing you to the depth of your soul, which is fundamentally 'you'. We examine the essential philosophies that underpin all our therapeutic work and how we view the individual person as paramount in that process. This work looks at how we focus on each individual's relationship to gaining self-insight, which is important to us because we aim to put the steering wheel of their transformation into their own hands, rather than wedging them into a certain theoretical perspective.

Chapter 3 describes some of the ideas that guide the Past Life Transpersonal Therapy approach and why it is so effective in helping create change. It may possibly challenge your current beliefs in the existence of past lives, suggesting also that delving into such a deeply creative way of working can bring you into powerful alignment. We explore how unresolved issues in your life can be linked to past life experiences, as well as introducing some of our spontaneous past life experiences with clients.

Chapter 4 explores the unfinished business that we hold in our present day, which can cause disruption in our lives. We help you reflect on your more deeply held issues and explore if they were born out of another life. Karma is introduced, illuminating how the lessons you have learnt and continue to learn are carried within you. We look at time and the important part it plays both in life and in the past life therapy method. Also explored is Carl Jung's 'collective unconscious', and inherited genetic memory, by way of introducing you to the theoretical and scientific ideas relating to how we know what we know and what we hold within us. We see how past life therapy can help you to create closures, find your purpose and meaning, and enhance your strengths and abilities.

In Chapter 5 we begin the journey into your own life, and past lives, considering who you are now, what aspects of living you are drawn to, and what you love to do in your life. Thinking about your meaning and the relevance of how you relate to other people, travel, places, and eras opens you to the realm of past lives and can creatively illuminate more about your current life.

Chapter 6 introduces quantum physics, and describes the store of Akashic records – all that you have ever thought, felt, or done. We explore the impact of the electrical energies you send out, and how to raise your inner vibrations to reach your intuition more effectively. People so often say, "I wish I had just listened to myself," but they don't quite hear what the message within them was saying because their vibrations were not high enough. We also present the different levels of consciousness, relating them to brain wave activity for understanding how to reach the depths of your consciousness through meditation and hypnosis, which is where your problem resolutions and healing can naturally occur.

Chapter 7 takes you into your own journey as we guide you through a past life visualisation. Here you will experience an exploration around the planet and through history so that you can find out more about you and your place in the world.

In Chapter 8 we continue through the stages of the actual process of Past Life Transpersonal Therapy. This includes the hypnotic induction, embodying the character, and exploring the past life to the passing over of that life. We clearly show you how to complete each stage and why you need to work through each part of the process.

Chapter 9 contains a real-life demonstration of how these stages are experienced and takes you through the beginning of a Past Life Transpersonal Therapy session. You'll read detailed feedback about the experience from the client, so you can see how the approach powerfully ignites someone's present day life to empower change.

Chapter 10 explores the further healing stages of the Past Life Transpersonal Therapy process, where your soul moves into the spirit realm for releasing and resolving the karmic messages and where the gaining of knowledge from the spirit guides, a greater understanding about your body choice and what you are here to do now takes place. Each part of the process is explained to help you understand how to use it in practice.

Chapter 11 gives you another important look into two further Past Life Transpersonal Therapy sessions, demonstrating the whole of the process that occurs within the spirit realm. It also includes feedback from the clients about how the sessions impacted their lives.

We close in Chapter 12 with our parting thoughts on this journey through the ages and the experience of *Healing from the Other Side*.

We want this book to be an experience that you can look back on throughout your life. As you read through the book, you will come across sections where we refer you to the accompanying workbook, marked with the following symbol:

These sections are designed to help you chart your journey of self-discovery into your past lives. The workbook, along with other support materials, can be downloaded at the book support website at www.healingfromtheotherside.com. We hope you'll take the time to engage with the exercises and the learning to be gained from them.

So join us now in the following pages as we step into the world of past lives and discover what you can uncover in your own past life journey.

Healing From The Other Side

~ **Part One** ~

'Somebody has *got* to tell.'
~ *Ken Wilber* ~

~ **PART ONE** ~

CHAPTER 1
THE WHATS, WHYS, AND HOWS

Until you make the unconscious conscious,
it will direct your life and you will call it fate.
Carl Gustav Jung

THE EVOLUTION

For many years our work delved into the intricate workings of the conscious mind and the realms of the unexamined recesses of the preconscious and the unconscious. We sought to unearth and then shape the 'out of awareness' unconscious forces that were seemingly driving ingrained beliefs and patterns of behaviours and thus the experience of life and living. In our first book *Thinking Therapeutically* (2010), we detailed various samples of our therapeutic work from a combined twenty-five years of experience. Our aim was to inspire others into the variety of different methods open to them when helping people move forward in their lives, such as hypnotherapy, Neuro-Linguistic Programming, and guided imagery.

Over the last few years our continued philosophical, existential, and phenomenological studies, our research into areas such as emotion and the body and our own ongoing personal development has directly led us full circle. We have returned to what fundamentally drew us both into the psychological and psychotherapeutic field in the first place. We have re-embraced what we already knew but needed to hold back from, partly due to being immersed in teaching the traditional psychological genres that needed to form the bedrock of our therapist training programmes. We began to experience a reconnection with a long-held awareness that, whatever the presenting issue or the symptoms being experienced by the people seeking our help, it is not only what lies beneath these that needs exploring. There are desires that remain often unexamined, yet which are inherent within us. These include the search for meaning and a greater connection with ourselves, along with the seeking for more of what is 'out there' in life. This can bubble away underneath symptoms, unhelpful habits and limiting worldviews, keeping at bay such deep and potentially overwhelming quests and discoveries. Asking questions of ourselves about 'meaning and purpose' is a big, and sometimes scary, deal! Often it is easiest for people to allow themselves to get immersed and wrapped up in day-to-day living. It's in no way a criticism; it is indeed entirely understandable. However, wondering what 'sense of purpose' one is meant to find and what it means to live fully, lingers below the feelings of dissatisfaction in some of the most fundamental aspects of life, like relationships, jobs and careers, financial matters and physical health.

The thoughts, feelings, and behaviours that people present to therapy, often makes the idea of personal freedom out of reach and incomprehensible. They distance the recognition that there are choices as to how we live our life and how we respond to what we encounter. The awareness of being responsible for the choices we make and don't make in this life becomes hijacked. The myriad of social systems that have been put in place add to this. They look to create order and control, guiding us into what is *supposed* to leave us feeling content, which is in fact leaving us potentially ever less autonomous, out of control, and drawn into a hopeless, insane quest to finding satisfying and enduring fulfilment. As Roger

Walsh and Frances Vaughan (1995) write, "We can never get enough of what we don't really want" (p. 348).

These are the struggles that can draw us away from feeling alive, and what can create a loss of one's sense of agency: the awareness that we can initiate, execute, and control our own actions and life in the world.

We see this loss daily in our work as many seek to relieve their symptoms via medication, clinically prescribed behavioural change techniques, and evidence-based, solution-oriented therapies. These methods initially appear to offer answers, but in reality, they lead to the asking of less and less pertinent questions about what the struggles that are being experienced might actually 'mean'. It is of course only natural that when somebody is experiencing inner unrest, unease, and dissatisfaction, that they first turn to symptom relief solutions. However, the importance of asking what is *underneath* these struggles should never be lost, else we are living an unenlightened existence, lacking in agency.

If we move past the problems we are experiencing and push back to the fundamental questions of living, we get closer to the underlying discord that is lurking beneath. The meaning of life, our sense of purpose, our freedom, the reclaiming of personal choice, and what it means to live fully are revealed. Here we see that all these wonderings are yearning to be acknowledged. A burning question within calls out for an answer. At some point in your life you may have asked it yourself. That question, often rhetorically posed, is . . . There *must* be more to life than this, mustn't there?

From an existential perspective, it has never felt completely comfortable answering, "No. That's it! That's your lot . . . so what are you going to do now?" It has never really felt to be a satisfactory response even though it confronts the individual to search within and challenge themselves as to what *is* therefore meaningful to them and how indeed they are going to live.

Why has it been disconcerting to hold such a view? Well, mostly because in the work we do, we see people grasping for more than finding a definitive answer or view of their own sense of meaning.

We so often see them searching for something else . . . for something more, not knowing what 'more' is, but searching nevertheless. We sense and feel them wanting to connect with more than what they cognitively know, with more than what they can touch, and see, and hear, and explain yet. They want deeper connections with themselves, with others and the world.

At a certain point the culmination of all that you know brings you to a place where you recognise that 'you don't know what you don't yet know' – and this is where our own search into 'the transpersonal' world emanated from. Our quest for 'outgrowth' and transcendence from accepted social convention, and scientific worldviews, fuelled a desire to examine beyond the 'personal self' and into higher levels of consciousness and connectedness. We located this in the transpersonal realm – as in beyond the individual person, to the idea of a higher self, a more evolved version of our self. Here we find the expanding of the idea of ourselves as not only human beings, but as spiritual beings.

Existentialist Emmy van Deurzen (1997) describes how people are "in search of a deeply philosophical ideology to underpin their lives" (p. 124), Through our work we also see them searching for something outside of themselves, something *otherly*. By fully immersing into that 'something else', we were drawn further into the realms of transpersonal psychology.

This wasn't such a transitional leap of faith as you might think. Our work incorporating the use of creative imagery and symbolism as a therapeutic method of discovery has, over the years, been extremely powerful and at times intensely inspirational and life changing – spiritually enlightening even. The depth to which somebody's innermost world can be explored through connecting at an imaginary level so often opens them to a world of intense realisations. This provides answers to long-held problematic behaviours and ways of being that conventional talking therapies simply struggle to find a vocabulary for or get to the roots of.

Our personal discussions in the last few years with some of the leading figures in the world of transpersonal psychology, such as Dr John Rowan, Dr Vitor Rodrigues, and Professor Jure Biechonski, have enabled our knowledge to deepen, leading to further spiritual enquiries that required to be nourished. Delving into Carl Jung's (1875–1961) mammoth volumes of literature and his notion of the collective unconscious, as well as Robert Assagioli's (1888–1974) work on psychosynthesis wetted our appetite. As we dug deeper, Stanislav Grof's (1931–) ideas on gaining insight and healing through the use of non-ordinary states of consciousness, has provided us with vast amounts of fascinating material to feed our continuous exploration. This has further illuminated what it is that beckons us in our search for greater connection.

With our existential studies and our continued discoveries within the transpersonal world we re-met with a passionate vigour the paradigm of past life regression therapy, a technique that we both knew well. We had used it over the years and found it to be incredibly effective in connecting those who experienced it to something more profound than anything they had tried previously. We became drawn into looking at and exploring with each other the whole subject of past lives from a deeper theoretical perspective than we had done so before.

Past Life Transpersonal Therapy – PLTT

In a deeper examination into the theoretical roots of transpersonal psychology, we began to formulate a more solid depth to the various aspects of past life regression therapy than we were accustomed to. We looked beyond the 'technique' and towards what was actually being connected with in the various stages of the process. We recognised that the method indeed drew from solid practical transpersonal ideas. These included the use of active imagination, the imaginal world (the subtle or intermediate world between the physical and the pure spiritual realm), Jung's collective unconscious, mythology, a higher self, guided fantasy, and non-ordinary states of consciousness, to name but a few.

Our own existential philosophy remained and continues to remain ever-present, in terms of the importance of exploring the notion of meaning and purpose and the essential nature of existence. However, the focus of the *theoretical* driver of the 'working parts' of past life therapy, for us, leaned most definitely towards the transpersonal world. We were acutely aware at this point in our work of the migration from the existential to the more transpersonal realm and how historically this has been cloaked in complications. Notions such as the soul, the higher self, and spirituality have classically fallen outside of the existential remit. As Existential-Humanistic psychotherapist Bob Edelstein (2011) writes, "Existential philosophers and psychotherapists have long been at odds about spirituality." Nevertheless, as Edelstein elaborates, there is a need to bridge the gap. He recounts a conversation he had with the renowned American existential psychologist Rollo May (1909-1994) at a conference he attended: "I asked if one could be both existential and spiritual. He *(May)* responded that it was essential to be both . . . Having an openness to life with its mystery, from ecstasy to tragedy, is spiritual whether you call it that or not" (2011).

For us as psychotherapists, with a deep commitment to the rigour of academia, May's words hit home. Life can indeed at times feel entwined with a spiritual energy and essence, whatever 'theoretical' doctrine one subscribes to. So to position past life therapy within a psychological 'home' it feels important to name its foundations, its theoretical roots, which comfortably align to the transpersonal, and thus our approach of 'Past Life Transpersonal Therapy' was born.

Our continued explorations led us naturally into considering varying states of consciousness, and eventually to the work of American author and philosopher Ken Wilber (1949–), one of the pioneers of transpersonal psychology and founder of Integral Theory. The exploring of Wilber's work has played a big part as to why this book exists. In reading the opening section of Wilber's book *Integral Psychology* (2000), we came across the powerful inspiration we were looking for that also provided insight into some long-held questions.

S = K LOG I, AND THE SOUL

Wilber describes during his research for a book on the history of psychology that at the time, most of the literature available pointed towards psychology and the psyche abruptly coming into 'being' around the year of 1879. But, as Wilber puzzled, "did the psyche itself just jump into existence in 1879" (2000, p. vii)? As he continued searching he unravelled a surprising historical 'severing' of psychology and the 'soul', as psychology began its migration into the scientific realms. This was attributed in most part to the work of Gustav Fechner (1801–1887), who at the time was one of the founding figures of modern day psychology. Fechner's insight (which soon became known as 'Fechner's Law') into a connection between the mind and body – on October 22, 1850 – was deemed as the solution of how to apply quantitative measurement to the mind. This in its simplest terms meant that for the first time, the world of science could measure the mind, rendering psychology 'scientific'. In psychology, is this indeed where the soul was severed from the psyche? It certainly seems to be the case, especially to one of the founding fathers of psychology at the time, Wilhelm Wundt (1832–1920) who proclaimed Fechner's 'discovery' as so, declaring, "Modern psychology has indeed assumed a scientific character, and may keep aloof from all metaphysical controversy" (2000, p. viii).

Wilber writes, "This Dr. Fechner, I presumed, has saved psychology from contamination by soul or spirit, and happily reduced the mind to measurable doodads, thus ushering in the era of truly scientific psychology" (2000, p. viii). The soul hereby appears to disappear from psychology as the scientific pursuit and measurement of the mind began in earnest.

A few years later, Wilber unearthed another of Fechner's books, entitled *The Little Book of Life after Death* (1835/1904), in which he was astonished to read a previously unknown philosophy of Fechner, entitled the *three* lives of the human being. As we read Wilber's words, we were overwhelmed as to the resonance 'three lives' held with the past life philosophies, and these ideas we were discovering took us together into a quite profound exploration. Fechner writes:

> Man lives upon the earth not once, but three times. His first stage of life is a continuous sleep; the second is an alternation between sleeping and waking; the third is an eternal waking. In the first stage man lives alone in darkness; in the second he lives with companions, near and among others, but detached; in the third his life is merged with that of the other souls of the Supreme Spirit. (1904, p. 1-2)

We both remember distinctly these opening words of Fechner's and were transfixed. What did this mean? At first, we couldn't fathom what Fechner was relating to, and so we kept on reading:

> In the first stage the body is developed from the germ and evolves its equipment for the second; in the second the spirit unfolds from its seed and realizes its powers for the third; in the third is developed the divine spark which lies in every human soul. The passing from the first to the second is called birth, the transition from the second to the third is called death. But death is only a second birth into a freer existence, in which the spirit breaks through . . . (1904, p. 2-4)

It hit us with a force we still remember. The father of modern psychology, the originator of 'Fechner's Law', the groundbreaking scientific formula (which incidentally is $S = K \log I$) that enshrined psychology into the world of measured science, was in fact speaking here of mind, body, and soul. Here was the evolution of consciousness through three stages, which included life after life, in the spiritual form. Wilber echoes the words that also ran through our minds at that point, "and why did the textbooks not bother to tell us *that*" (p. ix)? It was a moment that cemented our desire to write *Healing from the Other Side* and share this most important addition to Fechner's philosophy, because, as Wilber proclaims, "Somebody has *got* to tell" (p. ix).

Our belief is that from questions about living, such as one seeks when thrown into an existential crisis, answers cannot be found in simply becoming sure as to what we know. The enlightenment we pursue presents itself also in recognising that we are on a soulful journey, and *that* journey is an unfolding story as to how we have lived, how we live today and how our future might look. There is an abundance we carry within us – vast amounts of potential and possibilities – much of which comes from another time and another space. There are things we are here to do, and there are learnings we are here to discover as an ever-evolving being.

To fit us neatly into that which can be measured or evidenced would be to underestimate the enormity of your soul's journey through this life. We are more than any of us know, and we hope that in *Healing from the Other Side* you gain a greater clarity as to what that is for yourself. Our own journeys through past life therapy and connections with ourselves at a soul level has undoubtedly enriched our lives.

So, we certainly know that whether you are suspicious about the notion of past lives or can't quite get your head around the idea that existence is eternal, stepping into this realm, allowing yourself to connect to something other than you can explain, will improve the quality of your life. You will open up fully to *this* life, and that impacts your future more than it is possible to know. But don't just take our word for it. Here is an account of someone who has experienced the power of this work with us, with remarkable results. For the purpose of client anonymity, we have changed the names and any identifying details of this person, and the other clients in the sessions presented in this book.

An Experience of Past Life Transpersonal Therapy

Prea was looking to make a big change in her life. She had tried counselling but was still struggling to take the steps she needed to. Something was blocking her and she couldn't get to the bottom of it. She wanted to be able to end a relationship that both she and her partner were having difficulty bringing closure to. Even though they both wanted to go their separate ways, something was binding them together. Prea said that she felt like there was some unfinished business that was keeping them from splitting.

In Prea's past life therapy session with us (the transcript of the session is in Chapter 9), she went back to a previous life, being age 18 or 19. She was a young woman waiting for her husband, a soldier, to return home to where she was living in Japan. The year was around 1100. The boredom was so very painful, as all she had to do was wait for her husband. When we moved her life on in the regressed part of the session, she had a baby with her, a daughter whom she loved and who gave her much joy, but still, a sense of great unrest remained. One day soldiers came into the place where she was living and her child vanished. She wanted her husband to come and rescue her, but he couldn't because he had to fight elsewhere. As the soldiers set fire to the village, she felt totally abandoned.

The following is what she wrote about her experience, after this very session:

> "The life that I was being shown was strangely paralleling aspects of my current life experience. At the time of the regression, I was in a relationship that seemed to mirror some aspects of the life that I saw during the PLTT session. My present relationship had a strange connection and familiarity that I had not ever experienced in previous relationships. Also, it was a very difficult relationship that triggered profound insecurities and anxiety, which was destroying it. The more we tried to break away from each other, the harder it was to let go of each other. There was a mutual sense of unfinished business between us, which was very uncomfortable.
>
> PLTT showed me what my life had been like within this relationship in a previous lifetime. The events surrounding my death in that life seemed to have been carried forward in my psyche in this lifetime.

I had unearthed some information during the PLTT, so I followed it up with some research. I had a date and location along with clear imagery of the buildings, how they were constructed and so on. What I found out was astonishing. I found art work from that era depicting battle scenes similar to what I saw in the regression. I found historical information describing a feudal waring society circa 1200. I had a sense of myself wearing a white dress and I found a similar type of outfit and hair style in my researching that I had experienced in the PLTT.

This was really strange, but even stranger for me was a conversation that I had with my partner following the regression therapy session. I explained my experience of our relationship during the regression, how I had died alone, waiting for him to return. He then told me that he had actually visited a psychic, a woman who had recounted a past life to him. She had told him that she had died in medieval Japan after a battle, when she was a small child. She said that she had a clear memory of the events, described hiding throughout the battle and then finding her mother lying dead in a pool of blood. She described sitting with her mother's body waiting for her father to return, eventually starving to death. She had told him that he had been her father in that previous lifetime and that she knew they would meet in this lifetime.

What I found fascinating was that she could not have known my own past life experience prior to her revealing this to my partner. I had not even discussed the child part of my regression session experience with him. This additional information was coming from a third party and it answered my question of what had happened to the child. During the regression, I was deeply distressed about not knowing where the child was during the battle but now I had my answer."

LASTING BENEFITS FROM PAST LIFE TRANSPERSONAL THERAPY

Prea continues in her written account to discuss the effects of her experience:

> "The regression has changed me profoundly. I had always carried a deep and inexplicable sadness which I have been conscious of for most of my life. After the regression, I felt an almost instant release from the sadness, I felt that a heaviness had lifted from my heart.
>
> As time has gone by I have felt more confident, calmer, and more at ease with the world. I no longer feel worried about things that I can't control and am less anxious about outcomes.
>
> I have been able to finally find closure with my ex-partner and we have worked on our separation respectfully, without either of us holding onto any destructive residual emotions. I am convinced that these changes have arisen from being able to contextualise (what I believe to be) a deep and ancient memory, that has been tapping me on the shoulder for most of my life. From my experience during PLTT I have been shown the source of these residual emotions and I no longer feel compelled to re-live this experience. I have been able to release this and free myself."

We would like to thank Prea for writing this account for us and for allowing us to share this with you to show just how profoundly powerful these experiences can be.

If you have ever questioned whether you can dare to believe in past lives, Prea's is a true story, an account of her actual experience. Nothing here has been made up. You will read a full transcription of her session in Chapter 9 (and can access the recorded video session at www.healingfromtheotherside.com). The research she did after the session about the era, the place, and the clothing all just seemed to match the information she found. She had no idea about this time period previously.

Whether you believe in past lives or not, we have found over many years that these profound experiences that the mind can access or create (depending on your beliefs) will touch you deeply, so that you too can have a deep sense of understanding, release, and peace. We hope you'll find whatever *you* are looking for as we now step further into *Healing from the Other Side*.

CHAPTER 2
I'LL SEE IT WHEN I BELIEVE IT!

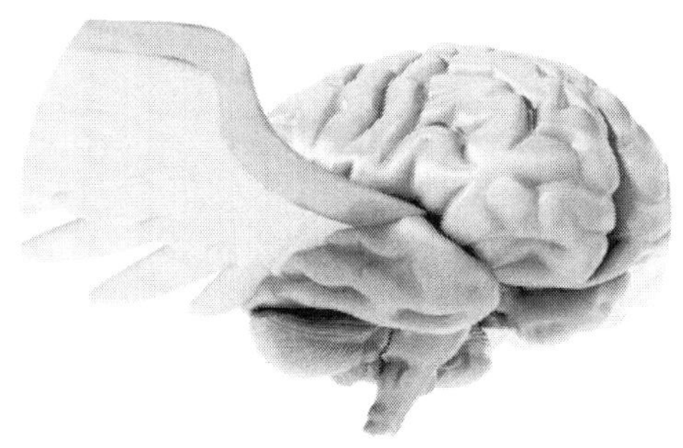

Beliefs are only a relative truth
distorted by all the knowledge we have.
Don Miguel Ruiz

BY NO STRETCH OF THE IMAGINATION

Muhammed Ali, aka The Greatest, once said, "The man who has no creativity has no wings." Indeed, it is in connecting with the power of *creative imagination* that Past Life Transpersonal Therapy offers such an incredibly rich learning experience, setting people free to aspire to all they can be. In this way of working, we begin by moving our focus from the outside world and what is happening 'out there' and guide ourselves intimately into our inner world. This is where you can truly meet yourself, open up to your intuition, and enter a place where you are able to share the stories you have inside you – stories that have been longing for a voice, sometimes for many lifetimes.

These stories convey your inner knowledge in a way that goes way beyond what you consciously think about, what you have been told, and what has happened to you. This moves you beyond the logical, and deeper into your awareness than can be accessed by normal brain wave activity, and into your inner wisdom – a multifaceted wisdom which draws upon, among other qualities, an embodied intuitive world of images and symbols. The renowned American psychologist and past life specialist Michael Newton, writes that without connecting with our inner wisdom, "we cannot truly be wise about how to live our lives today on Earth" (2009, p. 6).

In our professional experience of over forty combined years of study and research, one of the problems we see happening in clients presenting with a wide variety of emotional and psychological issues is a disconnection with their imagination. This is experienced as a loss of mental flexibility and a narrowing of consciousness which leaves them struggling in their present experiencing moment. They are shut off from accessing their deeper truth, and are repeating the same patterns with the same frustrating feelings. Even if there is a trauma from the past being re-experienced as flashbacks, it still becomes an all-consuming repetition in the present moment. This stuckness and narrowing of consciousness so often reveals itself when we suggest, "Imagine how your life would look without this problem." Frequently we are met with a surprised look, followed by their frustration and sadness at not being able to envisage life differently.

When it is difficult to access your imagination, the future becomes uncertain because you can't see anything different from how things are now. You can't creatively find solutions nor can you unearth the roots of what's happening to you. To foster changes we need to re-configure the tightly bound logical brain-mind process and excite the mind through an increased self-awareness and a heightened degree of consciousness. We need to re-ignite the inner creative juices in order to change those patterns and strategies which bind tightly to the symptoms being experienced. As Azriel ReShel (2016) writes, "We need our imagination to read something into things, to create images out of things and to make up stories for health and well-being."

In imaginative reflections and visualisations, we can consider the idea of being someone else, or a different (better) version of ourselves, and we can find a connection to the notions of meaning and purpose. The psychoanalyst Carl Jung described what this concept of allowing ourselves to imagine and fantasise through the 'active imagination' meant, that being where images take on, as Rowan describes, "a life of their own" (1999, p. 51). We can imagine ourselves both in the past and in the future. We can try on new ways of being and imagine holding different thoughts and realities while remaining present to ourselves. In this inner world, we feel how we would feel and are impacted as we would be, were the situation 'real'. In this way, the mind becomes more flexible and the holding of negative beliefs and emotions can start to realign, revealing to us a new perspective of our true values and giving us a deeper connection to our sense of self. In his TED talk in 2004, psychologist Mihaly Csikszentmihalyi said, "When we are involved in creativity, we feel that we are living more fully than during the rest of life."

Research is also showing the physiological benefits of becoming more imaginative. Heather Stuckey and Jeremy Noble (2010) considered more than one hundred studies on art, healing, and health. They found that there were a variety of positive outcomes from engaging the imagination, including a decrease in depressive symptoms and stress responses, an increase in positive emotions, and even improvements in immune system functioning. Learning to connect with your creative and imaginative capability is proving to be life-enhancing and even lifesaving.

This learning is not however something new, as we all develop an imaginative world as children. It is an essential part of our healthy brain development. We are encouraged to and naturally play imaginary games with each other, making up stories and acting them out through models, toys, and drawings. However, as we grow, there is a certain degree of *unlearning* that happens. Our creative imagination gets put to one side and becomes dormant through education, socialisation, gender role expectations, or with the toll of fitting into a world that rewards rational logic above creativity.

As children, using our creative imagination is commonplace and is indeed an important function in helping us deal with fears and anxieties. As May (1950/2012) writes, "It is well known that the anxiety of children (as well as of adults) is often displaced upon ghosts, witches, and other objects which do not have a specific relation to the child's objective world but do fulfil significant functions for his subjective needs" (Loc. 1626). In other words, these imaginary entities provide children with a way of dealing with real life anxieties and fears such as fractious relationships with parents or siblings. Whatever the shift of anxiety onto imaginary beings may be about, the imagination provides a very real alternative outlet for the fears and anxieties that the child is experiencing. Not convinced? Try telling a child who screams in the night at the ghost in the corner or the monster under the bed that they're not real and see how much it helps!

From children to adults, imagination is one of the greatest gifts of being human. It provides hope, helps us forget our troubles, and focuses us on what really matters and what is really important to us. Our imagination gives us the ability to create and express our inner world and find something that is beyond ourselves and that transcends our fixed sense of identity.

Past Life Transpersonal Therapy provides the key to a world of deep creativity. It takes us into our inner worlds in the 'here and now' and guides us to a whole new creative reality of the 'there and then' where we meet our higher self, our true soul, our wise intuition, and inner wisdom. It releases emotional blockages previously held in place by rational logic, and relieves our emotional brain from anxieties and fears, giving our rational brain greater freedom. It also helps us find the answers we need to live a full and purposeful life, this life, in the most creative way we know.

When people tell us they don't believe that past lives exist or that there is no empirical evidence – despite the vast amount of corroborated stories of past life experiences presented over many years – there is no need or desire for us to prove them wrong. This helps nobody. Their beliefs are their beliefs, and we respect their point of view, because in truth past life therapy doesn't require somebody experiencing it to believe in past lives. "You don't have to believe in past lives for past life therapy to work. The proof is in the pudding" (Weiss, 1995, p. 55). What is important however, is that they are open to the notion that they 'don't know what they don't know' and in that sense can open their minds to the potential, power, and possibilities that can be gained by delving into the depths of their creative mind.

In opening yourself up to your creative imagination you will be able to transcend your ideas about who you are. This is the only prerequisite to engaging in this work, as, in the words of American astronomer and astrophysicist Carl Sagan, "Imagination often carries us to worlds that never were. But without it we go nowhere" (1980, p. 4).

Let's Brain Storm

Of course, there is a lot more taking place within you when your imagination is active. Let's explore the brain itself now to understand further how past life therapy can bring your brain to greater life.

Neuroscience shows us that to change the way we feel, we need to become aware of our inner subjective sensing world and open up to what is happening on a deeper level inside (ReShel, 2016). The people we work with using Past Life Transpersonal Therapy are often intensely examining some aspect of their life, perhaps not understanding or being able to make sense of their thoughts and feelings. This process seeks to help enhance their awareness, connecting them more deeply to themselves and their purpose in life, with the discoveries from their past life experiences guiding them. Thus, this process connects the parts of the brain required for 'inner experience recognition' and the 'translation of this into words' – two different parts of the brain that can become misaligned. Let's look to understand this further.

The brain's main job is to ensure your survival. Away from our conscious awareness, the brain generates signals that tell us what our body needs, such as food or sleep. It creates a map of the world that helps us know how to get these needs met. It warns us of any dangers and opportunities along the way and can adjust our actions based on what is happening in the moment. As we can only survive and thrive well in groups, the brain also has to operate, participate, and co-operate alongside others. The psychological problems that can hinder people happen when those internal signals stop working efficiently, when our map of the world doesn't get us what we need or no longer makes sense, when we are too frozen to move (such as in a trauma), or when our relationships break down.

Every structure of the brain plays an essential part in the smooth running of all of these in life (Van Der Kolk, 2015). The rational brain – the neocortex (of which the frontal lobes are the largest part) – is about 30 percent of the brain and is focused mainly on information from the outside world. It looks to understand how things and people work, sets goals, and finds ways to creatively achieve them, such as imagining them in a future reality. Beneath the rational brain, in evolutionary terms, are two much older parts which are in charge of everything else.

The deepest part of our brain is involved with the real basics: hunger, tiredness, desire, excitement, pleasure, and pain. It monitors and rids the body of toxins, controls the energy levels of the body, and co-ordinates all the physiological basic life sustaining systems, such as your immune, respiratory, and endocrine systems. This is commonly known as the reptilian brain. Some of these basic systems can be neglected when you think about your mind and behaviour. They can be thrown out of sync when you are misaligned in some way, whether physiologically, psychologically, emotionally, or spiritually. Think of how many psychological problems involve difficulties with sleep, eating, digestion (IBS), and arousal (anxiety). What is really important is to be able to reach and address these basic bodily functions via gaining realignment and harmony through deep psychological connections and exploration. Lowering our brain frequencies and expanding our consciousness through PLTT offers this possibility.

There is also another part above the reptilian brain commonly known as the limbic system or mammalian brain (which all animals that live in groups possess). It monitors danger, deciding what is fearful and pleasurable and what is important for survival. It also manages living within social groups. This is shaped by childhood experiences and genetics, which contribute to our emotional and perceptual maps of the world. If we experience neglect, we come to specialise in managing feelings of fear and rejection. If we experience safety and love, we specialise in enjoyment, creativity, and curiosity.

The reptilian brain and the limbic system together make up the emotional brain. They look out for you and alert you to potential danger by physical signs when needed. For example, some of these physical sensations may be butterflies in your stomach for nervousness or tightening in your chest for panic, which draw your attention away from what you are focusing on. Imagine your own small reactions and how they direct the decisions you make, of when, what, and how much you eat, how much you sleep, what you like to do, who you like to spend time with, and how to evade situations you detest.

The emotional brain is simplistic and assesses these situations globally. So those cotton threads over in the corner . . . that could be a spider, or that moving pile of leaves in the road when you are driving . . . that could be a cat. Somebody standing behind you . . . might be a dangerous attacker, or that shadow from a tree . . . could be an ominous figure. You are instantly alerted through your bodily feelings because you may need to act quickly. Your mind has jumped to conclusions based on the 'better to be safe than sorry' principle. These reactions need no planning or thought; it is only later that the rational brain kicks in and has its say on the matter.

Let's go back to the outer part of the brain again, the neocortex (which is thicker in humans than it is in other animals). The frontal lobes give us words, the capacity to understand abstract and symbolic ideas, and allows us to plan and to imagine future scenarios. It underpins our extraordinary creativity and as much of it as possible needs to be active. As the distinguished psychiatrist Dr Bessel Van Der Kolk (2015) writes, "Without flexible, active frontal lobes people become creatures of habit and their relationships become superficial and routine. Invention and innovation, discovery and wonder – all are lacking" (Loc. 1026).

Ordinarily, the frontal lobes, which provide us with our rational decision-making skills, have the ability to override the emotional brain, meaning we don't *have* to eat when we feel hungry or shout when we feel angry or upset. It is in the edge between the frontal lobes and the emotional brain that we can access unlimited potential, but where also our psychological and emotional problems can begin. The stronger the emotional brain reacts, the less capacity the rational brain has to connect with our creative imagination.

What is important in the rapid gain of knowledge from the field of neuroscience is how the kind of creative approach that past life therapy offers, connects our rational brain with our emotional brain, and thus illuminates the path towards our deepest self. Here we can influence the parts that trigger our emotional reactions and can especially begin to calm any anxiety, panic, or trauma which are in need of soothing.

What also comes from this powerful realignment is the potential to enter a place of quiet contemplation, mindful listening, and deep body connection with a clearer awareness of your ongoing inner narrative. This will benefit your brain, increasing blood flow to your cortex by up to 10 percent. More blood flow means more oxygen, and more oxygen means the brain can work at its optimum level. This can lead to higher states of consciousness, greater vibrations, an enhanced sense of wellbeing, and improved emotional health. Brain, mind, body, and soul – breathing life into your life.

However, opening up to this creative connection, where the rational and emotion brain are working in harmony, isn't always plain sailing. As we have said previously, for many of the people we meet, the circumstances of their lives encapsulates them within the struggles of anxiety, depression, stress, habits and addictions, and a mindset where even the notion of change seems impossible. So how best then to help?

CAPTURING THE WHOLE PICTURE

During our careers, we have spent many years engaged in the process of psychotherapy in its various forms, as practitioners, teachers, academics, and authors. Psychotherapy offers a myriad of models and approaches, which are most often chosen to satisfy both the nature of the people that seek help and the theoretical paradigms aligned to the practitioners that use them. These include both cognitive behavioural approaches which are concerned with the impact of our thoughts on our feelings and behaviours, and psychodynamic models which are primarily concerned with the early development of the person and their psyche.

In addition, there are philosophical approaches to the person, such as the existential school of thought, which focuses on what it means to live, and models that are concerned with the essential nature of the human organism and its evolvement, such as the humanistic approaches. In recent times, there has also been much mentioned of evidence-based psychotherapy, which offers an 'instruction manual' approach to psychological healing. Heading in a very different direction is that which we have mentioned previously, transpersonal psychotherapy, sometimes referred to as spiritual psychology. This model, which we feel expands the experience of living, incorporates the spiritual and transcendent aspects of being human.

This very brief overview of the major psychotherapeutic approaches and their varying points of focus in healing, whilst not an exhaustive list, hopefully gives you some awareness of the different ways of considering psychological and emotional development.

Does it make sense to ask which of these then holds the key to human growth? Not really, because, in short, all of them and none of them do. We say this because, in our opinion, the human experience is as diverse as the realms that each of the approaches claims to focus upon, and thus each of them offers guidance on some aspect of being human.

Our own perspectives on human development draw on all the above theories, methods, and approaches, yet, for us, what holds itself firm as a fundamentally vital aspect of human growth and development, is an appreciation that we weren't designed to be positioned into any one theory of being. Resulting from our work in the psychological field, we have come to find, especially through our philosophical and physiological studies, that, beyond any one model, the single most influential force for change is the infinite and unending power of the creative mind. It is through this that we are able to meet the depths of our truest self.

As we have mentioned earlier, the imagination – and what is open to exploration within the realms of the 'imaginal world' (Miller, 1981; Rowan, 1993), that place where images and symbols open up our understandings in a different way than language and words do or can – holds infinite potential.

CONSCIOUSNESS

There is, however, a need to organise the way we approach the work we do, considering the multifaceted aspects of the human being we wish to help with the approaches we are looking to integrate. A major aspect of this consideration is the consciousness of the person we are working with, as this plays a large part in how they connect with their creativity. The *Merriam-Webster Dictionary* ("Consciousness," 2018) defines consciousness as "the quality or state of being aware especially of something within oneself." In order to access one's creative power, an expansion of consciousness, and thus a degree of self-awareness, is not only desirable, but necessary. What aspect of this inner quest for awareness does one then concentrate on? Classically, psychology hasn't made the point of focus in the search for enhanced consciousness easy.

As Wilber (2000) asserts in his calling for a more 'integral psychology', one of the problems of psychology is that, over time, the different schools of theoretical thought, such as we have mentioned above, have focused on their preferred aspects of consciousness. This has been to the detriment of what other aspects of consciousness have to offer in terms of understanding the human experience. Wilber (2000) observes this:

> Behaviorism notoriously reduced consciousness to its observable, behavioral manifestations. Psychoanalysis . . . to structures of the ego. Existentialism . . . to its personal structures and modes of intentionality. Cognitive science . . .

> reducing consciousness to its objective dimensions and biocomputer-like functions, thus devastating the lifeworld of consciousness itself. (p. 1-2)

Asian psychologies, such as the yogic and Buddhist psychologies of India, and the Taoist and neo-Confucian systems of China, "excel in their account of consciousness development" (Wilber, 2000, p. 2), especially when exploring the development of human beings towards a more transpersonal awareness. Yet, as Wilber adds, still something is missing in these philosophies, particularly in the formation of our crucial early life consciousness awareness and the evolution of an ever-developing sense of self. In applying Wilber's more integrated viewpoint, where aspects of *all* of the experience of a person are taken into account, we can bring new greater levels of awareness to what somebody is experiencing in their world. This is where past life therapeutic exploration is invaluable, as altered and expanding states of consciousness enable the accessing of new connections and increased awareness, which leads to deeper understandings.

What we have found helpful in our search for an integrated approach that incorporates various yet interrelated aspects of a person's world, is what Dr Roger Woolger, one of the pioneers of past life regression therapy, describes in his book *Other Lives, Other Selves* (1988) as the Lotus Wheel (Figure 1.1).

Woolger's Lotus Wheel shows the multidimensional aspects of the human psyche, especially the interrelation between the personal known aspects of consciousness in one's 'personal world' and the likely lesser known aspects of the 'transpersonal world'. It is through an exploration of the issue at hand via all these aspects that we can enable an exponential growth for those who travel this journey.

Towards the personal aspects of the wheel, which one might describe as the 'here and now' and what is 'known', are the Existential concerns that are commonly found: for example, in relationship struggles, where we come face to face with what really matters to us. The Biographical aspect of the wheel includes childhood memories and other memories that make up the 'story' of our life. The Somatic aspect carries the story of our physical existence and of our body in the world, including illnesses or bodily traumas, for example.

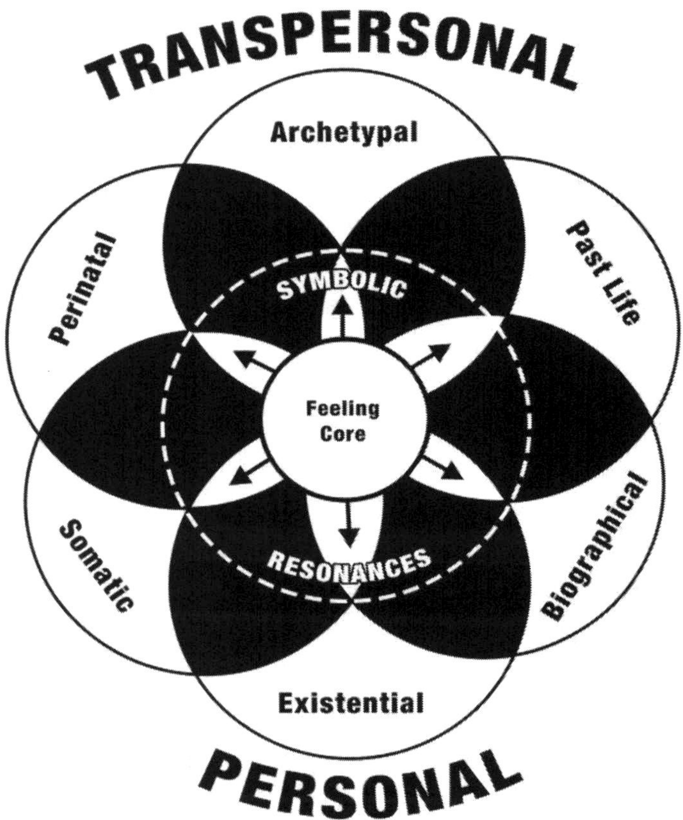

Figure 1.1

As we move towards the transpersonal aspects of the Lotus Wheel, we encounter the Perinatal that includes the weeks and months before and after birth. There is the obvious impact of the experience of growing from foetus to baby through to the birth experience and then the startling introduction to the world for the young child. Here we begin to connect with what has been brought into this life from a time before birth. Woolger (1988, p. 116) gives an example of the child in the birth experience getting the umbilical cord wrapped around its neck and formulating in those distressing moments the sensation that leads to ruminations of, "Do I deserve to live?" The Past Life aspect of the wheel is where the human experience highlights what we have brought forth into this life from past incarnations along with the karmic inheritance, the messages and learnings we carry to be faced in our current life. Finally, in the transpersonal part of the Lotus Wheel, we meet the Archetypal insights, enabling us to connect with the symbolic meanings behind the lessons we need to confront. Here we might uncover, for example, denial of the rebel, visionary, or explorer within us.

Woolger describes how "there is no need for any particular order of priority on the lotus wheel any more than there is a fixed starting point in any therapy session" (1998, p. 117). A body therapist might start instinctively, however, from the somatic aspect, a primal therapist from the perinatal aspect, a psychodynamic therapist from the biographical aspect, or the Jungian analyst from the archetypal aspect. The point is that all aspects are encompassed in life, and the journey of therapeutic exploration through them all can help with greater self-understanding, and in the seeking of what Woolger calls the 'feeling core' of the difficulties we experience. This being the place that we need to connect with for healing to take place.

In approaching Past Life Transpersonal Therapy with an awareness guided by all of the varying aspects of the Lotus Wheel, we refrain from positioning past life therapy as some kind of esoteric endeavor. We cement its rightful place as a therapeutic approach of tremendous benefit in the world of psychological therapy that we have worked within for many years. Let's step further now into the fascinating realms of transpersonal psychology.

The Transpersonal World

The distinguished clergyman, scholar, and social critic, William R. Inge (1860-1954), writes,

> Everyone has two journeys to make through life. There is the outer journey, with its variety of incidents and the milestones . . . There is also an inner journey, a spiritual odyssey, with a secret history of its own. (cited in Lovejoy, 2017, p. ix)

Transpersonal psychology has been described as exploring "experiences in which the sense of identity or self extends beyond (trans) the individual or personal to encompass wider aspects of humankind, life, psyche or cosmos" (Walsh & Vaughan, 1993, p. 203). It is within this context that we present this book, dealing with aspects of what it is to be human, that, as American psychiatrist and Jungian analyst Bruce Scotton (1996, p. 3) describes, are "beyond conventional, personal or individual levels."

Our use of altered states of consciousness (a major aspect of transpersonal concern), such as the utilisation of hypnosis within our work (Barber and Westland, 2010), made it inevitable that we would appreciate aspects of the human experience that transcend traditional psychological realms. An altered state of consciousness is a temporary transformation in one's normal mental state without being considered unconscious. It is widely appreciated that altering your conscious state, as occurs for example through meditation or relaxation techniques, has been found to benefit your health both in your mind and body (Fallio, 2007; Feuerstein, 2013; Shapiro, 2017).

In the late 1960's, the pioneering humanistic psychologist Abraham Maslow (1908–1970) described the transpersonal approach as the 'fourth force' in psychology (Chinen, 1996), distinguishing it from the three common traditional approaches of psychoanalysis, behaviourism, and humanistic psychology. The therapeutic model works with a number of key themes in seeking to understand the human experience. These include altered states of consciousness, a higher or ultimate potentiality, moving beyond the ego or personal self, transcendence of the self, and the spiritual domain (Lajoie and Shapiro, 1992).

In considering the 'self' – a combination of the transpersonal, self-transcendent (considering oneself an integral part of the universe), and spiritual aspects of human experience – the key value is that of moving towards wholeness through self-actualisation and self-realisation. Dr Vitor Rodrigues and Dr Harris Friedman (2015) describe transpersonal psychotherapies as being "based on the assumption that consciousness is at the core of what being human means. This defines the human broadly as being a physiological, emotional, intellectual, social and spiritual consciousness system in its totality" (p. 580-581).

The methodology involved in the process of transpersonal work consists of a combination of spiritual traditions from around the world which are integrated with elements of contemporary psychology. These look to understand such areas as our ambitions, loves, and concerns as we move through life, each calling us to uncover and then hold a deeper sense of meaning and purpose through the discovery of our deepest self. Some of the transpersonal methods include the use of body awareness and movement, holotropic breathwork, guided visualisation, dream work, regression therapy, development of the imagination and intuition, and symbolic art work to name but a few. It is this rich and varied drawing on multifaceted methods that helps inform so much of the work we do with past life explorations.

This powerful approach looks to foster greater human development, acknowledging that spiritual experiences and higher states seen in altruism, creativity, and profound connectedness to the universe, are universal human experiences. This culminates in a deeper integration of one's sense of connectedness with a higher-self (our truest form), other people, nature, and the entire cosmos (Kasprow and Scotton, 1999).

Therefore, we see past life therapy as residing in aspects of human experience more suitably aligned to transpersonal psychology. For some people the notion of past lives gravitates more towards the nature of the extrapersonal psychic, paranormal, clairvoyance kind of paradigm; for others, they incline more to transpersonal incorporations such as archetypes, the inner teacher, intuition, and creativity – which aligns with our own personal view. The British psychologist and psychotherapist Dr John Rowan writes, "Work with past-life experiences is sometimes closer to one and sometimes to the other" (1993/1999, p. 11).

As we explore such concepts as self, psyche, cosmos, potentiality, and self-transcendence, we are reminded of the very specific language that is found in the world of the transpersonal, and indeed in much of psychology. Such concepts might be unfamiliar and alien to somebody not versed in such terminology. This urges us to go back to the transpersonal that is found in everyday life so as to connect you to what you already know.

Rowan (1999, p. 13–27) describes aspects of our everyday living that show the transpersonal element in play, such as when we hear that *inner voice* warning us or giving us a hunch on an urgent matter. You may have experienced hearing the inner voice in those times when you say to yourself, "I just *need* to do this!" He also describes how we are connected to different kinds of *intuition*, such as that of a child 'knowing' something is wrong or the kind of intuition we rely on in groups in order to fit in and get along. You might best relate to this intuition as 'trusting your gut feeling'.

Additionally, Rowan (2001) explores how we can access different levels of *creativity* and open ourselves up to the various inner creative parts of us through playfulness, drama, writing, problem-solving, and other similar pursuits. Of course, accessing these parts of ourselves is often influenced by particular circumstances, certain people, specific times, and various places (we write further about this in Chapter 5). Finally, he describes the everyday living *peak experience* that can come through a variety of scenarios where we experience an 'at one-ness'. Watching a beautiful sunset, being captivated by a piece of art, becoming immersed in a moving piece of music, or even giving birth can all connect us deeply in this way.

These everyday examples show that the transpersonal world *is* your world. It is all you experience in those most utterly connected of times. Early pioneer of the transpersonal psychology movement, Dr Stanislav Grof, writes that transpersonal experiences involve "an expansion or extension of consciousness beyond the usual ego boundaries and beyond the limitations of time and space" (1979, p. 155). We see that both Woolger's transpersonal aspects of the human experience and Rowan's descriptions of the everyday *living* of the transpersonal elements, demonstrates how essential the transpersonal is in connecting us with the vitality of life.

THE IMMATERIAL

The nature of past lives conjures all kinds of positive and negative connotations. Some people, such as those growing up in parts of the world like India, consider past lives an entirely normal part of life. As children, they have often discussed their experiences of past lives in graphic, matter-of-fact detail. Many cases of children and adults alike are documented in books such as Carol Bowman's *Children's Past Lives* (1998), Tom Shroder's *Old Souls* (1999), Allan Botkin's *Induced After Death Communication* (2005), Roy Hunter's *The Art of Spiritual Hypnosis* (2016), and Bruce Koloski's *Your Journey Was Never Meant to End* (2017). In other parts of the western world, certainly pre-1950's, the notion of past lives has been ridiculed as nonsense, lacking empirical evidence, and the stuff of dreams and fairy tales. Who then is correct?

Maybe what is more important than an answer to that question is to engage in a deeper appreciation of the various past-life philosophies. By working to encompass not only the material facets of existence, such as measurable thoughts and behaviours, and considering also the immaterial aspects of life that the transpersonal illuminates, such as the existence of the soul and the notion of a higher self, we can get closer to a sense of wholeness in the experience of *being* human. As Wilber (despite Fechner's Law) aptly reminds us, "The word psychology means the study of the psyche, and the word *psyche* means mind or soul . . . the roots of psychology lie deep within the human soul and spirit" (2000, p. vii).

Whatever your understanding and view of all that we have explored so far, and however you connect to the various ideas that we present, it would be hard to deny the essence of something as fundamentally entwined with your human body as the soul. Indeed, so strong is the belief that a "human being is a composite thing, made up of two distinct natures, a body and a soul" (Baker and Goetz, 2011, p. 1), that a strong exploration around the *functions* of the soul leaves the idea of whether the soul exists or not very much falling by the wayside (see *The Soul Hypothesis*, Baker and Goetz, 2011). But first, what of such a notion as the 'higher self'?

DISCOVERING YOUR HIGHER SELF

As you began to enter this exploration of yourself through this book, you may have connected with different versions of yourself. Perhaps you have experienced a younger self within you with an inner voice that says, "I'm scared" or "This is fun", or maybe you have a parent version of yourself with a voice that says, "Don't worry, everything is going to be okay, let's see where we go with this". If more critical, the voice might be damning of you, "Don't be stupid, what makes you think this will work?" or perhaps you have met a future nurturing self that encourages you and guides you as to the steps you need to take. But have you ever connected with your higher self?

Sandra remembers in her journey being able to connect with a child version of herself that needed to heal as she was confused, distressed, and scared. She also at times connected with a wiser version of herself that knew more of how she really felt about aspects of her life, encouraging her to grasp hold of experiences with more vigour. Through time, she was able to work through her childhood traumas and free her child self so she was able to become curious, playful, and have greater vitality, then gaining deeper alignment with her higher vision. This ever-continuing process of embracing new life experiences and challenges continually reveals more to her about herself, life and its potential.

Tom also remembers as a young adult a connection with an insecure and confused child version of himself, but he was always able to hold a deep awareness of a wiser version – like a Gandalf type figure from J. R. Tolkien's 1937 classic *The Hobbit* – there to elevate and guide him safely and with a wise authority. Through time and self-development, his inner child reached the freedom to be himself, and his connection with his higher self grew stronger.

His therapeutic work and his writing is full of great wisdom and intuition with some playfulness thrown in!

We hope you can see from above that connecting with your higher self is incredibly helpful in gaining the most out of your life. Let's consider and understand further then what this means for you.

The higher self is the most evolved version of you. It is your knowledgeable self, with complete awareness and understanding of your truth in your present life. To meet your higher self, you first need to begin to connect with your true thoughts and feelings. This is not always as easy as people like to think, because you don't always have time to reflect on how you are feeling, and sometimes it is painfully revealing to do so. Also, if you have had challenges or traumas as a child or adult, you may have turned off or away from your own genuine feelings and therefore don't really *know* how you feel. But this is where you need to start.

Write a few words now about how you are feeling today, right here, now. Also, what sort of thoughts have gone through your mind as you were reading these words?

Was that easy or quite challenging? It is a good idea to keep a thought and feeling diary to help connect with the deeper aspects of your true self. If you can write something regularly about your thoughts and how you are feeling, then in time you will become more familiar with yourself and get to know yourself at a deeper level, forging a greater connection with your higher self. There is nothing you need to analyse and interpret, rather just describe in a non-judgemental way. Allow yourself to say, "Okay, so today I am feeling anxious, like yesterday. It is a tight feeling in my chest and makes me feel trapped. When I feel my anxiety I think about self-doubt and a lack of confidence", rather than, "I am anxious, what's wrong with me, why am I feeling this way? I'm such an idiot!"

As we said above, your higher self is the most wise and knowing you, giving you sound guidance in your life, offering you great knowledge and awareness. Your higher self always accepts however you are feeling and wherever you are at in your life and is always ready to give counsel and guidance so that you can connect with more of you and your inner truth. It will guide you through your past with the insights and understandings that you need. If you are struggling to let go and fully grieve for a loss that you have suffered, for example, your higher self can lead you to where you need to go in order for you to be with your suffering so that you can heal.

Your higher self connects to your soul and the spiritual realm of your awareness – guiding you to enlightenment within yourself. We become aware of our higher self in our own unique way. It could be an energy, a feeling, an image of yourself as perhaps a wise ancient philosopher, or a mother or father figure. At the end of this section you will find a visualisation that will help you meet and connect with your higher self in a way that's right for you. This can be an emotional experience if you have not connected with this aspect of you before. Knowing your higher self is the start of becoming aware of your soul and understanding your spiritual essence and nature.

The Lost Soul

Jung writes, "Being that has soul is living being" (1968, p. 26). So what is the soul? According to the *Collins English Dictionary* ("Soul," 2017), "Your soul is the part of you that consists of your mind, character, thoughts, and feelings." This definition, in our opinion, falls short of encompassing the totality of a human being, and by the very nature of attempting to define the soul, it is almost *bound* to fail as the soul refers to so much more. In both Hebrew and Greek (in the New Testament), 'soul' refers to 'life', whether physical or eternal in nature. Your life – your soul – the immortal essence of you, referring to all your innermost spiritual values and principles. It is what animates your body and guides your personality. It holds the enormity of your will and the intricacies of your intellect. Yale psychiatrist Dr Anna Yusim (2017) writes,

> Our souls are the blueprint we bring into the world of how we are meant to grow, change, evolve, transform and meaningfully contribute to humankind over the course of our lives. Once we learn to hear our soul's whispers and uncover its deepest longings, it will guide us to a life of meaning and fulfilment. (p. xxxviii)

For Wilber (2000), the work we undertake as psychotherapists is fundamentally connected to the human soul, rather than considering challenges and difficulties to be either behavioural in origin or related to negative thinking patterns. Human beings are infinitely richer and more complex than perhaps you have thought about before.

Past Life Transpersonal Therapy enables us to unpack all of this and move to realms of consciousness where we are able not only to meet this combination of complexities, but most importantly, we can connect to the soul, in order to discover more about its essential nature.

As Jung's quote earlier suggests, *soul* and *being* form an entwined nature of living, and this is nowhere more apparent than when working with the active imagination in Past Life Transpersonal Therapy. Through this method we encounter the nature of the eternal soul, which accompanies us as a constant companion, transported from life to life, not simply as a bystander, but, as Jung saw it, deeply connected within the fibre of our being. Through this work, we experience and enable the uncovering of the soul and its existence within us. As we embody this, we connect with something quite magical. This is captured most beautifully through Wilber's (2000) words, where he speaks of the soul:

> In its gentle whisperings, there are the faintest hints of infinite love, glimmers of a life that time forgot, flashes of a bliss that must not be mentioned, an infinite intersection where the mysteries of eternity breathe life into mortal time . . . this secret quiet intersection of time and the very timeless, an intersection called the soul. (p. 106)

As you will discover later in this book, the work that is done in the spirit realm in Past Life Transpersonal Therapy – the place that Newton (2004) describes as the "life between lives" (p. xi) – is where we fully engage with the soul as its energy becomes present for us on our journey. The soul carries with it, and teaches us, the learning from all past life experiences. It continues with us, helping us on the next part of our voyage though time. As we engage in the process of PLTT, we are able to merge mind, brain, body, and the energy of the soul (Collins, 2011) and through this engagement create the atmosphere for greater depths of experiencing in this life, and future movement from life to life with a nourished and revitalised awareness of both purpose and meaning. The soul holds the light that will guide us to what we need. Renowned shaman Fernando Broca sums up distinctly:

> When I think of the soul, I think of something pure; completely luminescent and perfect. It cannot learn anything because it already knows everything. It cannot grow because it is already in its most evolved form. So the process of making your ego, your mind and your conscience recognize the soul is a process which in spirituality is called "awakening or enlightenment." It is the recognition of the divine light within us. (cited in Yusim, 2017, p. 35)

Let's begin then to connect with your higher self and your soul. Please make sure that you are not going to be disturbed for a while – the experience takes around twenty minutes. First turn off your phone and any other devices that could interrupt you. You need to ensure that you are not doing anything else other than reading the guided visualisation, or listening to it if you prefer (you can access the audio download by going to the book support page at www.healingfromtheotherside.com). It is best to listen to the visualisation so you can truly immerse yourself into the experience and let it unfold naturally. Once you have started we advise that you keep going until the end. Settle back and allow yourself to become curious.

The Journey to Your Higher Self and Your Soul – The Visualisation

If you are reading the following script, you'll notice that we occasionally [. . .] pause for a short while . . . and then continue, just as in this sentence. This is to give you time to drift with the visualisation and see what comes up for you.

Okay, so, when you are ready, just close your eyes and take a nice deep breath in and simply concentrate on the following words . . . and that's all we want you to do . . . is to concentrate on your breathing . . . and as you breathe in, imagine that you breathe in a deep sense of calmness and peace . . . and with each breath that you breathe out, that deep sense of calmness and peace . . . just simply begins to flow through your body. As it flows through your body, just imagine that inner eye inside your mind gently beginning to close down, shutting out all stray thoughts and images that you simply don't want to interfere with how relaxed, calm, and peaceful you can become.

We want you just to allow that feeling to continue to flow through you. From the top of your head down to the tips of your toes . . . and then flowing from the tips of your toes and moving gently up through each different part of your body . . . and as you follow it, moving through your toes and your feet . . . and your ankles and your calves and your shins . . . as you follow it, you continue to focus on these words. Of course, you can be aware of the different sounds around you occasionally from inside this room . . . and maybe from outside . . . as you become aware of those different sounds, just knowing that the only sound that you really need to be aware of is the sound of your voice inside your mind as you read these words . . . as that wave of calmness and peace just simply flows all the way through you . . . through your calves and your shins and your knees and through your thigh muscles, and all around your waist and your hips, experiencing a wonderful sense of peace and stillness . . . continuing to move through you.

And in your mind, counting back through those numbers. Starting at any number you wish. Choosing a number and beginning to count backwards quietly inside your mind . . . and with each count down, noticing . . . noticing that as the numbers get lower, your relaxation becomes deeper. And as your relaxation becomes deeper, the numbers simply get lower . . . and lower . . . and that wave of calmness and peace just gently flows.

And then . . . then it moves right the way up through your lower back . . . and as it moves through your lower back . . . imagine it moving up through the muscles on each side of your spine and your body. Drifting through your whole back, through the muscles on each side of your spine, up through your middle back . . . into your upper back . . . and as it goes through your back, going back, it moves then through into your shoulders . . . and that feeling continues right the way through your back and your shoulders . . . and then down through your body . . . centring in your stomach muscles . . . and the whole of your body feels that wave of calmness and peace, just continuing to flow through you.

As calmness and peace continue to flow through you, just imagine you are in the most beautiful of places and it's the beginning of a brand-new day in this place that is your sanctuary. A beautiful fresh summer's morning is before you . . . and it is just before dawn is breaking . . . where you become aware of feeling most at peace . . . most calm. And right there and right now it is the beginning of a new sunrise and you are outside enjoying all that is around you. There is a gentle, warm breeze against your skin and the smell of the morning air. . . and the sound of birds waking in the distance and nature coming alive readying itself also for the start of a new cycle. And . . . as you stand for a moment and breathe in the atmosphere of peace and calmness and tranquillity, you can hear the sound of waves lapping up onto the shore of a beach nearby.

You begin to walk, feeling the ground beneath your feet, thinking that you'd like to enjoy the sunrise . . . and as there is a beach nearby, you know you can enjoy it even more there . . . as you can also listen to the sound of the ocean with its power and awe. As you approach the beach, you can see the waves gently washing up onto the sand and then moving back into the ocean . . . tumbling up . . . and flowing back down . . . in an infinite rhythm of waves.

Here you can look out to the horizon . . . the water and sky seemingly meeting in the distance . . . as you relax even further, soaking up the wonder of this place. Very gently you notice the first rays of the sunrise over the horizon; it is like the sun is rising out of the water. Small streaks of colour shine into the sky, as the sky begins to grow lighter and brighter with the growing dawn . . . and the light reflects onto the water filling the view before you with streaks of glimmering light shimmering in ripples, glistening like sparkles of golden magic . . . the colours from the reflection on the water, beaming into the fresh blue sky . . . becoming as one . . . as even the odd cloud floating by seems to soak up the beauty of the sunrise. It feels like this is a sunrise like you have never seen before, the most perfect sunrise there could ever be . . . the depth of the colours, the beauty of the sun rising, the glistening of the water, the clouds in the sky, the smell of the deep blue ocean, the taste of the ocean mist on your lips, the warmth on your skin . . . all one awe-inspiring vision before you. The wonder of a new day, the freedom of a new beginning. You close your eyes for a while, and it is like these enchanting moments move within you now, like a wave of wisdom, more beautiful and more powerful than ever before, bringing you aligned with the possibilities of a new beginning . . . as the sun continues to stretch far into the vastness of the sky.

And as you bathe within this experience, you realise that you are not only a viewer of all that is happening before you, but that you are a deep part of the beginning of this new day, you are an intrinsic part of the sunrise . . . and as you absorb the feelings of those radiating colours and smells and tastes . . . slowly all becomes clearer to you . . . as the rays of light shine down from the golden sun and reflect back up from the ocean, you become increasingly aware that you and the sun rising into the sky are one and the same. You are the sun . . . and the sun is you . . . and there is an incredible awakening within you . . . a sense of vitality and aliveness from within you now as you feel the strength of your one-ness with nature and existence. For you are the sun, and you are the ocean. You are the colours, the shades, the smells, and the tastes . . . you are the glimmering reflections, the light, the dawn . . . and all of this is you.

And as this deep and magical realisation becomes clear . . . you gain access into a special place within yourself . . . and it feels like you have always known that it is there . . . and as you look to your left or maybe your right . . . you see that the clouds and the sunlight have formed into a golden globe, that then morphs into an image that signifies utter freedom for you . . . freedom to connect to your inner knowledge and your truth. Some people see this globe transform into an ancient symbol or a very personal and significant sign that opens the way to your inner truth, while others find a scroll or a sacred parchment or a slab of stone containing etchings of ancient hieroglyphics. Whatever you find . . . reach for it and hold it as this is the magic . . . feeling its warmth . . . its energy . . . its power . . . and take it deep within you . . . take it deeply within you and feel it becoming part of you and begin to become aware of your mind opening into yourself . . . your inner world and your deepest truth. The powerful wisdom and knowledge you hold in your mind, body, soul, and spirit is now yours to learn from and to grow from . . . helping you to at last be . . . completely and utterly yourself.

From where you are, you can glance to the beach . . . from where you watched the dawn begin to rise . . . and where you were in awe of the beginning of the sun drenching the horizon with its bright and glistening rays. And now you find yourself standing on the beach again and you notice that the sun has risen high . . . high into the sky while you connect with the golden magic within you . . . of knowledge . . . of wisdom and your inner truth. And you are aware of the warmth of the sun, the cool gentle breeze, and the smells and the sounds of the new day dawning . . . feeling a deeper sense of peace and a more profound inner quiet and contentment than you've ever experienced before.

And as you look around you . . . you begin to see your higher self emanating from all that is there . . . the sun, the ocean, the sky, the magic, the sounds and the smells, and the atmosphere, your higher self emanates from all of it . . . forming in front of you . . . and when it has fully formed you look at your higher self, and your higher self looks at you . . . and you know who this is . . . you just know . . . as they are fondly familiar and you connect to those feelings of great trust and respect that engulf you and flow deeply and powerfully within you. As your higher self glides towards you, you feel the positive feelings that emanate from your higher self, sensing the energy and knowledge and wisdom that radiates from within them. You too move towards them as they towards you . . . your higher self and you ready to meet again and reunite with a great sense of love and happiness and respect.

As your higher self embraces you . . . feel yourself merging into the knowledge, higher wisdom, and enlightenment . . . and you know . . . you sense greater completeness and wholeness than ever before because you have found the higher guiding facets of yourself.

A conversation then happens between you, maybe through words that you share or maybe through deep feelings flowing between you . . . where you build love and appreciation for each other, creating a bond never to be broken . . . and you will now hear and be guided by this all-embracing knowledge and awareness of your higher self. For they are always there, ready and willing to guide you in your life . . . to show you the knowledge and wisdom that you have. Now breathe . . . breathe in the awareness and the understanding of everything you've discovered about your higher self and take that deeply within you.

And now you look back out to the ocean, hearing the waves rolling in against the shore . . . you look up into the blue sky and the clouds gently floating by and you become aware of the sun shining down warming your skin and as you see nature just as it is meant to be, your connection with your higher self opens to you . . . and with your higher self present, you allow them to guide you as you see your soul in the way that is right and true for you . . . and open your heart . . . to the images, senses, and feelings that your higher self provides . . . feeling the inner qualities of your soul, your true dreams and goals and desires, your deepest insights about yourself, your true feelings about who you are . . . right now . . . and what you want to accomplish in this lifetime . . . maybe connecting with your purpose or a sense of your purpose . . . or maybe you allow yourself to open up to an awareness of your amazing, beautiful soul. And maybe you see images of past lives that show the history and the quality of your soul . . . or maybe you can tune in and align to the energy vibrations of your soul as you become aware of the nature of your spirituality.

Become aware . . . embrace enlightenment, knowledge, and wisdom and know from this day forward you know so much more than you have ever known . . . and you are so much more than you thought you were . . . and you are becoming.

And as you now allow all images to fade, breathe in the awareness and understanding of everything you have discovered . . . everything you now know. And when you are ready, slowly, calmly, and peacefully allow your eyes to open and return to full awareness and alertness . . . empowered and embracing all that you are.

This is a very powerful visualisation and we have had many people become highly emotional at the meeting of themselves and the awareness of their lives as it has been lived thus far. Take a few moments now to record your experience. Again, if you'd like to record all of your thoughts throughout these exercises in the accompanying workbook, you can download this at the support page at www.healingfromtheotherside.com.

What was the sunrise like? How was freedom represented to you? What happened when you met your higher self and then your soul? How did you feel?

We would love to hear about your experience. So, please feel free to share in our dedicated Facebook group, which you can find a link to at www.healingfromtheotherside.com. You can also find there other readers' stories and meet some likeminded people. Whatever you experienced is meaningful for you in some way, and you may benefit from exploring this with somebody else on another path.

We have been on quite some journey in this chapter, from delving into the impact of the imagination, to the alignment of the rational and emotional brains. We've explored the various schools of psychotherapeutic approaches and their views on consciousness, as well as the need for an integrated and multifaceted view of the world of a person, as Woolger's (1988) Lotus Wheel offers. And we have stepped into the world of the transpersonal, connecting you with your higher self and your soul.

Gaining understanding into all of these areas enables an opening up of your creative imagination, and it is within this that a true unearthing of your purpose is found, and where making meaning of your life is possible. Let's now take the next steps on this journey, into you and your life.

CHAPTER 3
THE DEVINE AHA!

We cannot solve our problems
with the same level of thinking that created them.
Albert Einstein

BODY OF EVIDENCE FOR PAST LIVES

Probably the best known, if not *the* most respected, collection of scientific data that appears to provide evidence of past lives, comes from the work of renowned psychiatrist and past life expert Dr Ian Stevenson (1994, 1995, 2000). He collected over three thousand cases of children from all over the world who, without the use of hypnosis, recalled a past life. In order to collect his data, Dr Stevenson methodically documented the children's statements in relation to their previous life experiences. He then identified the deceased person the child remembered being and verified the facts of this deceased person's life that matched the child's memory. He even matched birthmarks and birth defects in the children to wounds and scars on the deceased, corroborated by medical records. His strict methods systematically ruled out all 'normal' explanations for the children's memories. These children supplied names of towns, villages, relatives, occupations, relationships, attitudes, and emotions that were unique to a single, dead individual. These people had existed and this could be verified, and they all died with unresolved issues.

Dr Stevenson devoted forty years to the scientific documentation of past life memories. Many people, including sceptics and scholars, agree that these cases offer the best evidence yet for past lives.

Your Past is Right There within You

In life, problems can seem to linger no matter how hard we work on ourselves. Issues such as phobias, anxiety, obsessions, low moods, procrastination, and relationship problems can be really hard to change. They stop us from having the confidence to be ourselves and from doing what we really want to do in life. So why is it that when we want to stop doing something or stop feeling a certain way, we simply just can't, no matter how much willpower we muster or therapy we engage in?

As we have said before, there are often disconnections and disturbances within us that hinder our brain, mind, body and soul from being aligned. Fixed, habitual patterns of responses keep us away from the deeper connections we need to have with our meaning, purpose, and our soul. It is in reaching our soul that we find what is there and what needs to be understood and healed.

Within the past life context, our soul enters our current life with unfinished business from our past lives. Because this unfinished business remains ever present in our current life, we experience it both in the difficulties that we are seeking a resolution for and in our continual striving for freedom and peace. Some of the strongest patterns and recurring life themes that we have become aware of in our work have been eradicated once they have been connected to unresolved matters from past lives.

Give Me a Sign

There are a number of indicators that connect us to the experience of past lives. These include:

- Recurring dreams that take you back into another century or focus you on a particular place you have never visited and yet feels familiar.
- Déjà vu experiences.
- Precognition, in which you can accurately predict future events. This is sometimes referred to as future sight.
- Retrocognition. Knowing information about a past event that you practically should not know about.
- Feeling older than your age reflects. Feeling like a wise, old soul.
- Possessing a great affinity for certain cultures, time periods, and environments. For instance, you may have an inexplicable fascination for Egyptian culture, feel really 'at home' when in Scotland for no particular reason, or you are drawn to the nineteenth century.
- Unexplainable fears or phobias (other than your parents having a similar fear or phobia).

Unresolved Past Life Issues

As we were writing this book, we heard of Louise Hay's passing on 30th August, 2017, at the age of ninety. We had already intended to mention her work in this chapter, but it feels even more fitting to acknowledge her tremendous contributions to the world through her books and teachings, and her passion for demonstrating the mind-body relationship. If you've ever read her famous book, *You Can Heal Your Life* (1984), you'll appreciate the influential power your thoughts have over your emotions and physiology. In Hay's book, she describes how old, unresolved issues in our lives can re-present themselves through physical discord and illness. For example, neck problems arising out of a refusal to see alternative points of view, alongside stubbornness and inflexibility; indigestion being gut-level fear, dread, and anxiety; or asthma demonstrating the feeling of being stifled, unable to breathe, and suppressed crying.

In past life therapy we consider this very same notion. Unresolved issues from past lives re-present themselves in the present day as symptoms or situations for us to resolve.

Woolger, in his book *Healing Your Past Lives* (2010), describes present day problems as carrying "residues of previous lives still carried deeply in the psychic system we call the unconscious or the soul" (p. 11). Woolger also describes in further detail in *Other Lives, Other Selves* (1988) how past life traumas can lead to present day difficulties such as insecurity, depression, guilt complexes, eating disorders, and sexual difficulties, among others.

Let's think for a moment about some possible scenarios.

Present Day Symptoms/Behaviours	**Unresolved Past Life Connection: From Any Era**
Intrusive or obsessive thoughts. For example, cleanliness, checking or ordering things.	The thought connected to something meaningful in a past life. Hand washing could be coming from being in the trenches in World War I.
Finding it difficult to connect with people (for fear of losing them). Finding it difficult to be apart from someone (separation anxiety). Anxiety and depression.	Painful separation from family members, friends, or soul mates in a past life. As a child, being left alone or being orphaned. Living a downtrodden or restricted life.
Feeling that you are fundamentally an angry or sad person and have always been that way.	Unresolved feelings of anger, sadness, loss, frustration, and other difficult emotions from betrayal, desertion, or unfairness in a past life.
Always looking for a cause to fight for.	A need for retribution against those who did you grave harm.

Finding yourself in situations where you are unfairly treated and you struggle to let go. Overwhelming desire to make things right or to right a wrong.	Perhaps being left or deserted in a dangerous situation. Being led into war or betrayals. You may have harmed someone else in a moment of madness, a misunderstanding, or an accident.
Feeling great guilt and shame even though you know at one level you have done nothing wrong. Feeling you are a bad person.	The harbouring of guilt and shame of not standing by a promise or pact with or for another. "It's all my fault" from a past life situation such as leading troops into battle.
A repeating sense of doom at various times of year, such as anniversaries, seasons, and changes in daylight hours.	Incomplete final dying thoughts, feelings, desires, or wishes.
Death anxiety. Sense of foreboding. Waiting for something to go wrong. Finding you have a lot of physical problems.	Sudden or unexpected death in the physical form. Injury, malnourishment, or prolonged illness.
Fear of going out or taking any risks. Creating catastrophes in your life.	Violent and traumatic death.

What would it be like to discover how you can resolve issues that seem to have *always* been present in your life, even when you have no idea why? The phobia that you feel you were born with because you *always* seemed to have had it. That obsession that you just can't get out of your mind and for which there is no reason for it to have developed. The anxiety or guilt that never goes away, day or night. How would you feel if you were to find out how to break those deeply entrenched patterns that really make your life difficult? Imagine experiencing deep healing and resolution of these unresolved issues more quickly than with other more conventional therapeutic approaches, bringing you the peace and grounding you long for. We have both experienced how, in uncovering past life material and discovering the reasons behind present life difficulties, past life therapy offers a way to achieve all the above and more.

So what of the people we have worked with? For me, Tom, the whole idea of past lives was literally stumbled upon many years ago in a therapy session with an unsuspecting client. This is how the story went.

The Spontaneous Past Life

Tom's Experience

Dave came to see me to quit smoking, many years ago. He was absolutely huge! He towered above me at around six feet eight inches, and had come directly from a building site, where he had been bricklaying all day. He walked in demanding, "I want *you* to stop me smoking." And I replied somewhat stuttering my words, "Yes, okay . . . take a seat." I wasn't going to argue, and he wasn't taking failure as an option. So he sat down . . . well, just managed to edge himself into the chair, and waited for the session to begin.

At that time, it was quite early on in my career and I used regression therapy a lot when working with clients for all kinds of presenting concerns, such as we've written about in *Thinking Therapeutically* (Barber & Westland, 2010). I had been taught to use regression therapy to help people stop smoking. I was regressing them back to the first time they ever had a cigarette so that they could re-live that moment. If you've smoked, you'll remember that first cigarette . . .

it's basically like you feel you are going to die – because you're literally suffocating yourself.

So . . . I thought I would regress him to that experience and re-live it. This would highlight how unpleasant smoking is, and also his old – no longer relevant – reasons for smoking, breaking the pattern, and thus removing the need for smoking in the future. This was my theoretical perspective and it had worked very well in the past with other clients. This approach, which is a kind of aversion therapy, has gradually been succeeded with more elegant methods and thankfully kinder ways, using a combination of hypnotic suggestion, metaphors, and visualisations to enable people to successfully become non-smokers.

I started to regress him, and suddenly as I'm going back through the regression process, back to his first cigarette, his face became suddenly contorted. I looked at him and said, "What's going on (not really knowing what else to say). "I'm in some strange place . . . " he said, with his voice tone totally different. I said, "Tell me about this strange place." I was intrigued! And he said, "I'm . . . I'm like five or something . . . " and he started to describe being somewhere that sounded like the Midwest of America. He had sandals on and just a sheet tied around him with some cord or rope. It was hundreds of years ago, and his name was different. So I said, "Tell me more." And this big, strapping guy physically transformed, becoming smaller and sounding younger, as clearly what he was describing was not from this time. Not from this life at all.

So we went through it, through to his death as well, where he was being suffocated. A slow suffocation – which is not really that far off from the process of smoking. And then as we reached the end of this part of the session I said, "Okay, you can open your eyes now." And he opened his eyes and he said, "What the heck was that?" I said, "You know what . . . it sounds like you've just experienced a past life." Then he said, "What on earth is that!?"

So I explained it to him. Of course, he had no concept of what past lives were. No idea. Why would he? It just wasn't in his context or vocabulary. He'd never explored anything like that before. From that moment I knew I needed to know more.

Sandra's Experience

For me, Sandra, I also stumbled upon a spontaneous past life with an unsuspecting client, reminding me that it really doesn't matter if the individual believes in past lives, or is expecting to explore a past life or not; it can still happen out of the blue.

I was teaching a workshop early in my career on analytical hypno-healing. The basis of this approach is similar to Louise Hay's work, helping the client link specific physical symptoms with the emotional/psychological cause. In analytical hypno-healing, we look for the roots causing the condition, often found in the past.

Susan had terrible lower back problems. It meant she had restricted movement and was also in severe pain. She was on the maximum pain killer dosage and was still struggling. You can imagine she was very willing to take part in the practical session, once I had covered the theoretical aspects of how hypno-healing worked.

She sat there in front of the group visibly in pain, describing how this was impacting her life. She was tearful as she considered how this might be her future as well. I then took her into hypnosis and explored the area of pain, getting her to describe what it looked like before then saying, "In a moment I will count to three and snap my fingers and you will go back to the first time you experienced this pain . . . one, two, three." [*snap*] "Where are you?" There was a long pause and a frown came over her face. "What's happening?" I asked, wanting to quickly find out where she had gone back to and what was troubling her. "I don't know," she said. "I am a young man fighting some other men."

This wasn't what I was expecting at all, and clearly by the tone of her voice, neither was she (as you can imagine). She continued to tell me that they and she were not speaking English but wasn't sure what she was speaking. I was expecting her to go back to when she was aged five or six and perhaps had fallen out of a tree, or a time when her parents had separated and the burden she felt at being stuck in the middle. This certainly wasn't where we were. I gathered further information about where she was and what was happening there, realizing that she had obviously spontaneously regressed into a past life. She had gone back to being in some kind of civil war in another country, fighting, and it was here she lost her life by being speared in the back, exactly where the pain she had described earlier was.

After we had finished the session and she opened her eyes, she burst into tears. She was overwhelmed by the intensity of the experience, the connection to her back problem, and also the fact that she was feeling much less pain and could actually move easier. Something had instantly shifted in her and in a follow-up session, she said that her back certainly felt very different.

How can we explain stories of people who do not know about past lives or who are definitely not expecting to regress into a past life, suddenly experiencing and describing such things?

Of course, in this type of work, it helps to be curious and to have an open mind. But as you can see above, it's not essential. Just like anything in life, if you want the most out of it, it helps if you wonder about the potential possibilities of what you can experience. It is not essential to believe in the method you use to make the change you want but it is helpful. We have seen countless people over the years who were complete sceptics about the use of hypnosis who, after only one session of hypnotherapy, became non-smokers or overcame a lifelong phobia. We've both had some incredible experiences using PLTT, and to this day are amazed at how it opens people to more than they could ever imagine.

A past client, Simon, was terrified of heights, unable to get close to a window on the first floor of a building or climb up flights of stairs without having extreme panic and anxiety symptoms. In going through a session of past life therapy, he uncovered the reasons for this from a previous life. He understood why he had been afraid of heights for his entire life as he went back to dangling over a castle wall and clinging on for dear life, eventually falling off and dying. From there he released the trauma and resolved the experience, taking from it many learnings about his life and his outlook. Immediately after the session, he actually got onto a chair beside the window, looked out from the second-floor room that we were working in and stayed there, a smile beaming across his face. This took place in one of our training workshops, so there are many witnesses of how he was reacting to heights before the session and then watching him amazingly get up onto a chair and look out of the window. This is something he would never have contemplated as possible before. In fact, soon after beaming with glee, he burst into tears of relief as the realisation of a new way of life began to unfold in his mind. In the follow-up, fear of heights was never a problem again; it was no longer an issue in his life.

We've had people give up smoking, break free from their issues with money, become more energized, find they have reduced symptoms of ME, lessen back pain, form more intimate relationships – all from experiencing past life therapy. Esteemed colleagues of ours report similar such experiences (see Avraam-Repa's 2013 interview with Dr Vitor Rodrigues). It is an approach that offers a definite path for personal growth and healing. We have seen it happen right before our very eyes. It's a life changing experience.

We hope you are beginning to feel even more curious about the therapeutic journey into past lives and what it can unblock, because we want to make a difference to *your* life. We want to expand your mind and your world. This is the reason we write books, create self-development programmes, and teach workshops – we want to help you gain greater understanding of your inner and outer worlds. We want you to be able to connect to yourself, others, and the world at a deeper level than perhaps your experience now.

We couldn't possibly think of anything better to do with our given time here than help people overcome challenges that stop them living a complete and fulfilling life. It's the culmination of forty years of therapeutic experience behind us and a combination of thirty years of psychological studying in this life that goes into all our work, and creates what we hope you will find is an informative and uniquely powerful process.

Some time ago, we had no idea how we were going to start this book, but we just knew it had to be written. Now, we're really excited to be with you on this journey.

Insider Information

If you have ever had counselling or therapy, you may have experienced what we call the 'Aha moment'. This is when you realise something about yourself, about others, or the world that you didn't know before. For example, just recently one of Sandra's clients, Steven, who works in the emergency services, was exploring why he was having anger outbursts when he felt rushed into making a decision or when something happened that was unexpected. Even though he worked incredibly hard, he was finding that in trying to avoid being angry he was being held back in progressing in his role and consequently was missing promotions. His Aha moment came when we connected his present reaction to how he had come home from being away (when he was a teenager) and was rushing to the hospice to see his terminally ill father. As he threw open the entrance door, his mother caught him and told him his father had unexpectedly died two days previously. Not only did he have to take in that news, but if he wanted to view his father's body to say goodbye he had to do it right away. A big decision had to be made, and so the first dead body he saw was that of his father, for which he was totally unprepared. You can see the direct connection about not wanting to be surprised by anything and then feeling angry if he is rushed into making decisions. "Oh my goodness, that's it, isn't it. This makes so much sense," Steven said, as he burst into tears of sadness, but also tears of relief now that he knew what he had actually known somewhere within himself all along.

In an Aha moment the penny drops and all becomes clear. You certainly can't unknow this knowledge once you know it, and strangely when it is brought into awareness, there is also a sense of "Well, I did actually know that." From this point, something shifts within you, and the problem that has gripped you for so long loosens itself, shifts, and its power fades away. Simon's anger subsided from that moment in both his professional and personal lives.

CATERINA'S AHA MOMENT

We asked a good friend of ours, Caterina Farkash, a uniquely intuitive Family Constellations therapist if she would be kind enough to read the manuscript of *Healing from the Other Side.* Caterin travels the world demonstrating the power of inherited energy and the process of healing through uncovering historical family representations. We knew from the time we had spent with her that she has an amazing life story and wondered where she sat with past life regression. Catarina agreed, and replied to us with the following feedback, which she has kindly allowed us to share with you. It is a wonderful example of the Aha moment, experienced by a wise and insightful woman who dedicates her life to helping others achieve their own Aha moments through her work.

> "As I began to read the words from *Healing from the Other Side*, my memories of seeing and understanding the meaning of some of my own lessons in this lifetime came flooding back.
>
> A few years ago I decided to finally have the courage to overcome my unexplained opposition to past life therapy and find out what the approach was all about and what meaning there was in it. I began to learn all about the subject, remembering that as a student the best way to learn anything is by experience.
>
> In one of the lessons I discovered that there is a connection between how we die in a past life and how we are born in the next one. In my past life session, I saw myself as a little girl running happily in a big sea of yellow plants swaying in the wind. I could not hear any sounds, but was aware of the smells and feeling the sun and the wind. Next I found myself inside a big room, where there were many women and children making strange and scary faces that I had never seen before. I sensed I was clinging to my mother's legs and all I could see was all these people with scary faces and open mouths, trying to climb somehow higher and

higher with the children holding onto their mothers . . . and then slowly . . . everything disappeared.

For the first time in my life I realised that this scene was a replaying of the last time I died, in a gas chamber in a concentration camp in the Second World War . . . and that I did not realise that I was dying. This had a big impact on me.

Why this was so relevant to me in my current life was that both my parents were Holocaust survivors, and I was born one year after the Second World War ended, but I was born dead. After two days of hard labour I arrived, born as a dead baby, at only 1.9 kilograms. The doctor "put you in the garbage" my aunt told me. However, a cousin of my mother's, a doctor himself, was present at the time of my birth. He had lost his whole family in the war, including his wife who was nine months pregnant. He knew the history of my parents and all those that were murdered in Auschwitz and he simply could not let me die. So he began to work on resuscitating me, working tirelessly to 'resurrect' my tiny suffocated breathless body, until he miraculously succeeded. And so thankfully, here I am.

The connection I gained from this experience spurred me on to use past life therapy in my own Family Constellations work, to great effect. In one of my workshops the issue was that the person I was working with could not "find a place" where she wanted to build her house, her home. Her overriding thought, to which she had no explanation, was, "I have no place, I have no home." We agreed to use past life therapy as it was becoming more difficult to get to the bottom of this, and after a very short time, she saw herself in a previous life as a little boy, running with other little boys from their village, because white strangers had set their house on fire, with all the family inside. He witnessed his whole family burning and knew then that everything was gone. This led to an answer and subsequent solution to the current belief for the woman, as it now positioned that thought pattern in another lifetime. On her way home in the evening after the workshop, she called me and told me that she spoke to her husband and they had finally decided where to build their home.

I have many other examples like this also. Past life therapy is such an important aspect of our work, and everything that helps to unearth what is stuck in our stories is welcome. Thank you Tom and Sandra for your wonderful work."

We want to thank Caterina for sharing her story and hope this furthers your interest in how PLTT can lead to life changing Aha moments. When we look at life within the context of past life therapy, where we are souls moving through an eternal continuum of time, then we've been touched by many life lessons already. We know such a great deal that we don't yet know we know. These Aha moments, unearthed in past life therapy, powerfully bring huge relief as they are from our deepest inner world.

Just think about being touched by eternity and how much knowledge you have from the many, many life forms you have experienced throughout time. There is a wealth of not-yet-known knowledge you possess that can influence you and help you to make the changes you have been wanting and waiting to make. Exciting times lay ahead.

CHAPTER 4
THERE WILL BE AN ANSWER

You are exactly where you are meant to be.
Teresa of Ávila

CASE CLOSED

For many years now, we have been considering the importance of the notion of open and closed loops. An open loop is where we leave things unfinished and thus hold it within us, out of mind, yet lingering in the background of our life. For example, you have an argument with someone that is not resolved and you then don't speak to them. A year goes by and you're still not speaking, but you think about them often, wondering and pondering on how they are and what happened between you. Or maybe you started a course a while back, wanting to improve your knowledge of a particular subject, yet never finished it . . . but always intend to. These are open loops and amount to unfinished business.

We each carry with us a sense of our personal unfinished business, stored away in our inner mental filing cabinet. When we take time to explore it, find out what it is, and work to bringing a close to those matters, it can really change our lives. Simply by closing an open loop we can free up our mind and body space and focus more on present-day living.

When we first came across this idea, it had a huge impact on both of us, so we started to adopt the process of finding and closing the various loops in our lives. The difference it has made has been quite profound. It was like taking back control and becoming much more available to our present-day lives, minus the baggage.

So, over to you. If you think about your life as containing open loops, what feels like unfinished business for you? Perhaps something to do with your parents or a sibling? Work? Friends? That course?

Just think about it, and jot down a few things about what feels unfinished or remains open in your life at the moment. We shall revisit this in our explorations later on in the book. Head over to your workbook now at www.healingfromtheotherside.com and record your thoughts.

Closing open loops can create dramatic shifts in your life, as it has done for us. If you really want to know what to work on to free up your life and help you be more present and alive, this is it: close some of those open loops. Be honest with yourself and consider those times when you have said, "It really doesn't bother me" or "I've dealt with that", because these are often the phrases we use to try to minimise matters that do in fact still bother us, as they have not been dealt with as well as we might want to think.

It's useful, therefore, to just take one at a time, close the loop, and then look at what else is there. It can affect not just your whole life in a big way, but also the little things, such as the way you leave your house, the manner in which you greet somebody, or the way you finish a conversation with a loved one. We believe that one of the biggest learnings that will come out of discovering how to do this, is a new sense of freedom and space.

Often the open loops or unfinished business is within our relationships. If we look at Prea, whom we introduced you to in Chapter 1, her open loop was not being able to bring closure to a relationship. There was unfinished business keeping them together. In her past life it emerged that this came from never knowing where her husband had gone and why he didn't rescue her and their baby. In that one session she gained insights into what was binding her to the relationship, which created the potential for change. PLTT can really help create understanding, find closure, or provide the insights that help with creating closure in some aspect of our present-day lives.

You Don't Know Your Own Strength

It might be sounding at this stage as though we're saying past life therapy is a panacea, and simply sorts out what is wrong in your life and fixes your problems. Well, yes, it can do so. But another benefit of using past life therapy is that you can also illuminate your talents, abilities, and your calling. It's not all about solving problems; it's also about discovering possibilities, potentiality, and fostering growth.

Everybody has one or more unique and special abilities and talents. It may be in mathematics, helping others learn, being a parent, running a business, building/making things, or in music, art, acting, sport, or anything else. We all have things that we naturally find easy to do or be. For some people this is difficult to identify and fully own in this life, but in recognising and experiencing it in a past life it increases your awareness and ownership of your innate talents in this life.

So now it's over to you again. Take a few moments to think about what you find natural and easy to do. Things that you quickly become absorbed in and excel at. Again, make some notes in your workbook.

You may never have thought about it or written these down before, or you may have frustratedly struggled to write anything at all. We are so often *told* what we are good at and what we are not so good at, and when we take this on board we disconnect from our true sense of ourselves, our *own* awareness of our abilities and talents. When Albert Einstein, who revolutionised physics with his General Theory of Relativity, was age sixteen, the head of his school wrote about him in a damning report: "He will never amount to anything." Fred Astaire was once handed a note saying, "Can't sing. Can't act. Balding. Can dance a little." Thankfully, some stay with what feels right deep inside them. Dame Judy Dench, Harrison Ford, Van Gough, Michael Jordon, Marilyn Munroe, Richard Branson, and Walt Disney (and so many others) all stayed aligned to themselves and continued with what felt natural to them, despite being told they'd never make the grade. Many of us sadly heed what the deemed experts tell us, and give up. We put our dreams to one side and get on with living an average life, disconnected from our soul's infinite ability.

There's something incredibly empowering about knowing your abilities, and knowing where these abilities have come from and why they are pertinent to you. When you use past life therapy to do this, you gain a greater connection with your soul and discover a more solid base from which you can experience your authentic self. Once you have this greater sense of knowing really who you are, the ability and talent(s) that you have can be felt deeply within you and be fully embodied and embraced. Imagine for a moment how that would feel.

Why do we ask you to do this? Well, do you have in mind something that you do well but shrug it off as nothing special? Do you tell yourself that anyone can do that, or say that you have merely learned a skill rather than believing that your ability is something that is innately within you? If so, we want to challenge you on that. If you can come to the realisation that you do indeed have special, unique abilities or talents, with a firm belief that it is your exclusive gift . . . then guess what you can do? You can grow exponentially; other abilities will also become apparent to you and you can then own them too. You set a new solid and immovable foundation for your ever expanding and improving life.

Allowing yourself to engage with this kind of self-exploration in general, and more deeply in PLTT, can illuminate why you are in the place you find yourself in life, why you do the things you do, and why you are as you are. That can lead to an avalanche of incredible discoveries, profound inner growth, and a deeper sense of self ownership.

It's About Time!

Time plays a significant role in past life therapy. We use time distortion in the hypnotic induction, as well as regressing through time to the past life experience. As we explore past lives we move between experiences of times old and past. But it is not just in this process that time is so important. Indeed, time plays a significant role in the experience of life and living. The Spanish writer and philosopher Baltasar Gracian (1601-1658) once wrote, "All that really belongs to us is time; even he who has nothing else has that" (2017, p. 69).

The nature of time is so entwined with being human that it permeates every facet of life. We see time situated in historical references and common language. We read of 'ancient' myths and 'futuristic' technology. We speak of 'many moons ago', 'bygone eras', 'long lost empires' and experiences that seem to 'go on for eternity'.

The subject of time played a large part in Sir Isaac Newton's introduction to *Principia* (1687/1846), arguably one of, if not *the* most important, science books of all time. Newton carefully distinguishes between absolute time and common time. Absolute time (the 'real' time in Newton's opinion) is the same for everyone, everywhere in the universe. So, someone standing at the North Pole on Earth would experience time exactly the same way as someone standing on Mars.

Common time is that which Newton considered we are able to perceive, such as what can be observed in motion, like the Sun or Moon, and the ticking of terrestrial clocks. From these we measure the everyday passage of time, yet the perspective of time can be different in relation to where we are in the world, and what is being used to measure the time. It is subjective.

Indeed, one of the central figures in modern philosophy, Immanuel Kant (1724–1804) in his seminal work *Critique of Pure Reason* (1929) argued that time is not real but is a mental construct.

This was expanded on by another of the most influential figures in twentieth century philosophy, Martin Heidegger (1889–1976). His ground-breaking philosophical work *Being and Time* (1927/1962), looked at, among other things, the nature of time in relation to human existence.

In literature, fairy tales often include an important event that must happen 'before the clock strikes twelve' (Brun et al, 1993). Week in and week out millions of sports fans experience 'time distortion' as they wait out their team's last few crucial minutes in that weeks' match. Those on the winning side experience time frustratingly seeming to slow down and those on the losing side wait nervously for that last gasp goal, try, touchdown, or home run, feeling time slipping away faster and faster. Famous films such as *Back to The Future* (dir. Robert Zemeckis, 1985), *Groundhog Day* (dir. Harold Ramis, 1993), and *The Lake House* (dir. Alejandro Agresti, 2006) all centre around a magical movement through time. And of course, one of the most popular and longest running UK television shows ever produced, *Dr Who,* entertains us through the exploits of time travel.

Be it science, philosophy, literature, sport, or entertainment, time continuously fascinates the human race and entwines its mysteriousness within every aspect of living.

Neuroscience and Time

There have been many theories as to how the brain measures and creates our sense of time and the feeling of time passing (Hammond, 2013). Unlike clocks, where time is divided over specific intervals, the brain has no one single process of time measurement. The neuroscience of time-keeping is showing most recently that the neural circuits in the brain can wire themselves so that they can keep all sorts of time. This is crucial, as, with the different sensory information – sight, sound, touch, taste, smell, pain, temperature, balance, and body awareness – being processed at different speeds and by different areas of the body, the brain faces quite a challenge in creating a perception of time.

On a day-to-day basis, we each experience circadian rhythms, a kind of internal clock of sleeping and waking that governs the daily rhythms of our lives. The physical, mental, and behavioural changes that follow a daily recurrent cycle over roughly twenty-four hours (Vitaterna et al, 1994) is impressively precise. During this time, patterns of brain wave activity, hormone production, cell regeneration, and other biological activities can be clearly observed. These circadian rhythms are controlled by a part of your brain called the hypothalamus, and can not only be influenced by time, but also by other factors such as lightness and darkness. For example, when it gets dark at night, your eyes send a signal to the hypothalamus indicating that it's time to feel tired. Your brain, in turn, sends a signal to your body to release melatonin, which then makes your body tired.

As we have mentioned previously, the purpose of the brain is to ensure our survival and thus it is crucial that we are able to somewhat predict the future. Indeed, American neuroscientist and psychologist Dean Buonomano proposes that "the brain is a machine that remembers the past in order to predict the future" (2017, Loc. 279), and thus has the ability to travel back and forth in time. So we possess the ability for mental time travel, as well as a personal internal clock that guides us through life.

In therapy, a client may be asked to explore moving through time in order to create alternative imagined futures (James and Woodsmall, 1989). Time distortion, as we have said, can be used as a way of enhancing the outcome of hypnotic techniques (Battino and South, 2005). Also, exploring how a client relates to time and their inner and outer time consciousness can be the focus of exploration around their essence of 'lived time' (temporality) (Heidegger, 1962; Minkowski, 1970). Time, and how we perceive it, influences just about every experience we have. As British author and psychology lecturer Claudia Hammond (2013) writes, "Time perception matters because it is the experience of time that roots us in our mental reality. Time is not only at the heart of the way we organize life, but the way we experience it" (p. 11).

When life feels like it's uncomfortably rushing by, it is often because we are misaligned. There is an underlying desire beckoning us to meet our calling and 'be' who and what our destiny has scripted for us, yet we are ignoring it. But when we calmly feel that time is in plentiful abundance, then we are more likely on our intended 'path' and we feel fully alive, present to the world, open to all its wonders, mysteries, and surprises. PLTT works in helping you realign to your true path, slowing down your personal time, and connecting you more deeply to your life.

Our psychology plays an important part in influencing how we think, feel and behave in relation to time on a day to day basis. The finite nature of one's current life form, from the time of conception/birth to the time of death, is viewed in vastly different ways, from person to person. Some people prioritise taking as much time as they can to relax and enjoy life. For others, there is a need to cram as much into every day as they possibly can. So how is it for you? Does it feel like you've never enough time? Or does everything seem to take forever in your life? Do you feel aligned in time or does time run away with you? Maybe you feel like you're always waiting for something to happen, with time drifting by.

Write a few thoughts and feelings in your workbook or journal.

Let's take a moment to explore how you hold a sense of time within you. Take a watch or clock and choose a time at which you are going to close your eyes for two minutes. If need be, make a note of when you'll start. You're going to keep your eyes closed for what you imagine is exactly two minutes. When you think you're done, open your eyes and make a note of how much time has *actually*

passed on the watch or clock. So when you're ready, close your eyes and begin.

Okay, welcome back. Record the time you kept your eyes closed for.

So, how long was it? Exactly two minutes, or less, or much more? This very interesting exercise is one we often use when working with groups around the idea of time. Some of the group members, following the exact instructions you just did, will open their eyes after about thirty seconds, thinking two minutes have passed. Others take much longer. One person we remember taking nearly a full ten minutes! This illuminates so well the difference between our personal I-time and clock time, and shows how the mind can get seemingly lost in time.

In truth, we all have the exact same amount of time in a day as everybody else. As the famous quote by author H. Jackson Brown Jr reminds us, "You have exactly the same number of hours per day that were given to Helen Keller, Pasteur, Michelangelo, Mother Teresa, Leonardo da Vinci, Thomas Jefferson, and Albert Einstein." So, if we all have the same amount of time, why do we experience it so differently? Why does one person feel like there's never enough time and another that there's too much? Why does it feel that our long-awaited summer holiday flies by in no time at all, yet when we reminisce about the experience afterwards, it feels like it lasted far longer than when we were there? Known as the "Holiday Paradox" (Hammond, 2013, p. 7) this temporal illusion, just like the questions posed above, show that our "subject sense of time is precisely that – not objective" (Buonomano, 2017, Loc. 935).

With awareness of our ability to mentally 'time-travel' and the subjective nature of time, our work with clients using hypnosis utilises the experience of time becoming distorted, not through any particular method (although this is possible too; see Cooper and Erickson, 2002) but through the experience of entering into different states of consciousness. It's not uncommon for a client who has been in trance for forty-five minutes to think it was only five minutes. This can be attributed to the nature of hypnosis, where a dual state of consciousness occurs in which you are able to enter deeply into the realms of your unconscious mind and your past, or future, whilst at the same time clearly conversing, describing often a richly detailed and highly emotional journey through a dialogue with your therapist.

In conclusion, opening up to time as more than a linear construct, where sixty seconds equals one minute, sixty minutes equals one hour (and so on), and embracing the subjective nature of time and our abilities to mentally time travel is incredibly freeing, especially therapeutically. As Einstein proclaimed, "the dividing line between past, present and future is an illusion". So then, reality is timeless.

A Parallel Universe

Have you ever heard of someone talking about living in a parallel universe or having parallel lives? A good fictional account of this is the film *Sliding Doors* (dir. Peter Howitt, 1998). The film follows Helen, who has just been fired from her public relations job. The plot then splits into two parallel universes, based on the two possible paths her life could take, all depending on whether she catches a train or not.

In the first universe, she catches the train, meets James, and strikes up a conversation with him. She gets home in time to catch her boyfriend Gerry in bed with another woman, and she dumps him. In the second universe where she misses the train, she hails a taxi instead, but this time she gets mugged when a man snatches her handbag. Helen hits her head in the scuffle and ends up in hospital. She arrives home late from the hospital, giving the woman in bed with Gerry time to leave, and thus is oblivious to what Gerry has been doing. In both universes she ends up in the same hospital, but for different reasons, where in one universe she dies and in the other she recovers, seeing flashes of the 'other' Helen's life.

This film reveals this alternative view of the nature of time as it challenges us to suspend for a moment the belief that time exists as a singular linear process. We are asked to adopt the notion that time is multi-layered and exists on a continuum. Helen's parallel lives were happening simultaneously. If we consider time outside of our normal comfortable understanding and instead see time as a continuum – past, present, and future all joining and meeting – as do many cultures outside of the Judaeo-Christian tradition, both from ancient times to present day (Hart-Davis, 2011) – we can consider how any life could also be a past life *and* a future life, all being experienced simultaneously. This is a view held by many scientists today, who are of the opinion that all time exists simultaneously, a concept known as 'space-time continuum'.

Philosophically, the idea that time does not pass, but that time simply *is*, is not a new idea. As far back as the fourth century, theologian and philosopher St Augustine of Hippo (in the eleventh book of his *Confessions* (397-398 BCE/1970)) declared that the past and the future are mental constructions that we are only able to see through 'a window of presence', which we might call the 'now'. Aristotle (384-322 BCE) argued that "time cannot have had a beginning, since the first moment must have come between some bit of past and the future, and therefore could not be the first moment" (Hart-Davis, 2011, p. 20). Physicists also have long disagreed with the notion that time is segmented into past, present, and future, which is further echoed in religions such as Buddhism and Hinduism.

So, if you can suspend the idea of time as a linear construction of past, present, and future, then it's possible to explore yourself through your past lives, just as if they were this present life. You could also consider the potential of exploring future lives as well, as your present life runs parallel with them (see Jirsch, 2011, 2013). This presents us with a tremendous opportunity for re-evaluating our current life experience. How? And what do we open ourselves up to in this? Expert in Akashic records (which we explore in depth in Chapter 6), Sandra Anne Taylor (2016) describes the potential further:

> the past, present and future are happening simultaneously but resonating at different vibratory levels . . . the ever-present now, is happening at a much denser resonance. Our past falls away in a less dense vibration, while our future plane opens up in front of us. Our experience of sequential time is that linear moment. We are always in the 'now' in terms of what we see and feel. All the while, the rest of time is vibrating as pure potential in our lives. Past, present, and future all happening simultaneously offers a significant tool in dealing with our recorded codes and patterns. This gives us the opportunity to rewrite the records of the past, to choose consciously what we record in the present, and move forward to script the recorded details of the future. (p. 44)

In resolving and healing within one particular life, you will in essence be impacting *all* your lives. Where you are now, in this present life, exists alongside other lives of yours happening at the same time. It's a lot to take in, but in doing so you expand the potential and possibilities you are able to experience.

In past life therapy, step by step you discover what needs to be resolved 'then and there'. This doesn't happen just the once. That means that if you resolve unfinished business in another life, then that resolution has an immediate impact on *this* life from that very moment onwards. You're going to start doing things differently and thinking and feeling differently. It really does elicit an empowering awareness, knowing that you can go back and change things from your current life which will impact both then *and* now and will open your future lives up to further experiences and learning.

KARMA CHAMELEON!

We are both old enough to remember *Karma Chameleon*, the 1983 song by English band Culture Club. The song speaks of the fear of alienation and thus not standing up for what you believe in. In not being true to yourself and in not being how you really feel, Karma will pay you back. Alicia Keys, in 2003, also wrote a song called

Karma about a lover who gets what he deserves after letting her down. Both songs describe karma with a tone of retribution. Keys' first line of the chorus, "What goes around, comes around" is perhaps one of the most well-known (but not strictly accurate) interpretations of what karma is (Hadalski, 2011).

When someone who has treated you badly in the past has something negative happen to them we might say "that's karma for you", or if someone has treated you unfairly, you may hope that karma will pay them back for what they have done. However, karma isn't all about punishments and being paid back for the bad things we or others have done (the idea of cause and effect – for a deeper exploration of this see Humphreys, 1995 and Sion, 2010). We carry karma continually within us, influencing our thoughts, emotions, and actions, and we continually accumulate both good and bad karma throughout our lives to continue into the next.

What is Karma?

The origin of karma comes from Sanskrit, an ancient Indian language, and it means 'action, work, or deed'. It is our energetic history of all our past actions (cause) that influence our present and our future (effect).

> Karma is very often defined as the workings of the Law of Cause and Effect, but it's really the vibrations of our accumulation of choices, conclusions, and emotions that become part of our personal record. (Taylor, 2015, p. 22)

Let's consider the benefits of thinking 'karmically', as these are the foundations that for us shape the very landscape of Past Life Transpersonal Therapy and just in themselves can help us live a more fulfilling life. Firstly, we hold the view that we are responsible for the way that we are in the world and that we 'are what we are' due to our previous actions – and that we are always living within this dynamically. Secondly, our actions and the consequences of them are not fixed. We possess free will to choose what we think, feel, and do in any particular situation. We may feel compelled to do something which produces a relevant effect, but if we genuinely explore and are open to understanding these impulses we can change future actions. Thirdly, we need to focus on 'who am I becoming' rather than 'who am I'. Thus, we are looking to continually see things in a new light and to feel things in different ways. This resonates very much with French existential philosopher Jean Paul Sartre (1943) who describes how we 'become already' what we seek to be.

It is due to karma that we come into the world as we are – this is our karmic inheritance – which is what we bring from our past lives into this life. This is then continually being influenced through our family, home, friends, and the situations we find ourselves in, as well as the actions we have taken and not taken. Simply put, every thought, emotion, and action comes only from the past impressions that we carry within us (karma) and creates further karmic imprints. Karma will always be in your life now and in your future lives.

Karma gives us space and time to become more. One of the most fascinating things within the notion of karma is that it often shows us what we need to know in not so obvious ways, and sometimes ways that initially cause suffering. For example, some significant others who are karmically connected to you (and you to them) may switch appearance to help better the understanding of the karmic message. Thus a parent may have been your child in a former life or your current partner may have been a sibling. As you moved into your current life, the souls agreed to take on the opposite parts, so they switched roles and maybe genders. This is all part of the nature of eternal learning, as such positions shift throughout lifetimes based on karmic need. The main point is that whatever dynamic is needed to reveal karma, it will be manifested through changing roles and situations in our lives on earth. This means that the people you now know may have had a very different impact on your previous lives.

Take a moment to consider if you have ever met someone purely by chance or know someone close whom you feel strongly that you have known for more than a lifetime? Are you trying to end a relationship, but it is just so difficult to go your separate ways? Record a few comments about your thoughts.

Through these philosophies, we can see how we can easily begin to believe that we are therefore bound up in karma, but it is important to be reminded that we are not 'stuck' in karma. If someone is born into an un-resourced family or born into poverty, this doesn't mean that this is a permanent situation. We can lift ourselves up and out of that situation. If we engage in some meaningful self-exploration where we are being true to ourselves, we create movement and good karma, achieving greater balance.

This means that in understanding our karma, we are working towards being a person of greater depth, value, and wisdom. This endeavour leads to a deeper self-understanding of the karmic patterns we are creating and how we are influencing and creating the fabric of our lives. So, even if you disregard the past life view, just by embracing the notion of karma in your life, you will live a more fulfilled, accomplished, and positive existence. Embracing this can point you towards learning from your mistakes and thus lessen your suffering that is perhaps perpetuated through the replication of deep-seated habits. You can look to influence the energy that you put out into the world and in doing so change the future returns that you get back. However, it's only in honestly facing what's happened to you in your life, the unfinished business and the lessons that you can gain from these that you can settle within your karmic learning.

If we all have karma and are all acting from within our own karma, we undoubtedly influence other people and they us. This takes us to thinking about the bigger picture. As poet John Donne (1988) puts it, "No man is an island." Your karmic energy will not only be influencing your own actions but will also have significant consequences in the lives of others, and thus we are all collectively affecting each other.

We mention this because a question that we have often been asked is that if you have been abused or neglected as a child, or assaulted or experienced a trauma as an adult, are we saying "that's bad karma for you" and that you are being punished for something you have done in the past? No, far from it. We need to not think of bad karma as punishment. Karma just 'is'. No child deserves to be abused no matter what may have happened in their previous lives. But something *is* being created for you to work with and work through and find meaning in for yourself, at some point in your life.

Jung (1968) considered that those who have been violated have been given an opportunity to bring greater consciousness to mankind because they own a large piece of the very darkest of the collective shadow of humanity. For some this may offer understanding of their suffering and allow them to move forward in their lives confident on what they need to be doing. For others it may not.

We feel that whatever happens to us is a chance to illuminate our karma, rather than it being bad karma that brought this action upon us. What is fundamental here is what you do with what has happened now. How you transform your suffering and thus yourself from what has happened: this is what connects you with your karmic message.

In looking at your life story through personal meaning, something inevitably shifts you to greater self-connection and self-consciousness. Even if you don't find the answers (just yet), just by engaging in the search you are becoming a more enlightened being and your karma is changing. This is a journey into what your karma illuminates and the awareness of the choices you had (or didn't have) and what you did with those, and most importantly, what you do with those now. So if you have suffered a great deal in your life, it is a case of exploring just what you are struggling with in what happened to you. Then move towards the idea of enlightening yourself as to what the real resolution needs to be for you right now, to change or balance karma. How can you use it to make your life, and maybe the lives of others, better?

If you don't change your karma and it becomes stuck, then you will forge a karmic groove which will compel you in some way to repeat the circumstances, driven by the residue of unfinished business. You may repeat it in this life and will in future lives if not resolved.

If you want to move towards liberation and freedom, one of the first things that you need to do is to become more connected to the messages being carried in your karma, as otherwise no movement can happen. Past Life Transpersonal Therapy is certainly a way of gaining greater wisdom for yourself here. You see, karma repeats itself time and time again, attempting to teach you to do something different. If you're attracting the same controlling partner into your life over and over again or if you always find you are continually being walked over, it's time to stop and inspect your choices. Climb out of the ridges of that karmic groove, and look to resolve the karmic message so that you can move on and choose somebody different, someone more aligned to you.

This doesn't make previous partners in unsuccessful relationships bad people; they were a necessary part of your life's learning. They carried an important message for you and you for them. Woolger (1998) sums it up well:

> Unless we bring to the consciousness and detach ourselves from these latent compulsions, the past life complexes will continue to drive us to repeat circumstances and scenarios of old defeats, betrayals, losses, humiliations, violations, deprivations, injustices and so on. (p. 142)

The important point to make about karma is that it is influenced by *you*. Karma is neither something that happens to you nor is influenced by luck. It is impacted upon by your every decision, thought, word, and deed, both positive and negative (Hadalski, 2011).

How Do You Influence Your Karma?

In looking after your physical, emotional, and spiritual health, you are creating good karma, and good karma can create insights and meaning, which creates further good karma. In neglecting yourself or being angry, bitter, or resentful about something or someone and acting from this place, you are creating bad karma.

Traleg Kyabgon (2015) explores working with karma by prioritising our actions. Firstly, we can reduce negative karma by refraining from actions that are most harmful, such as becoming overwhelmed, self-deprecating, or finding self-destructive ways of managing ourselves rather than focusing on what we can achieve. Think of some things you can let go of because they cannot immediately be attained and list things that you are worrying about that you genuinely can't change. In letting go of these, we stop avoiding or focusing on things that create bad karma for ourselves.

Refer to your workbook now and consider the following points.

For good karma:

- Take a few moments to make a list of the things you can let go of.
- Consider some of the bad habits you have gradually accumulated over the years that are not helpful for you in your life, such as those that stop you connecting with yourself and others. Begin to create good karma by making small changes within these.
- List some good actions with good outcomes that you do or could do.
- How can you take care of your physical body a little better?
- Where can you verbally express yourself with more confidence and clarity?
- What could you do to enhance your creativity?

If we look at past life karmic philosophy metaphorically, karma is the suitcase your soul carries on its trip from life-to-life, the karmic impressions being carried over from one life to the next. Your soul contains all of your past lives, your hopes, dreams, regrets, traumas, relationships, which are yet to be fulfilled. It is based on the spiritual principle that what we didn't resolve in our past lives is karma which is carried within the soul, and will re-present itself in another life in some shape or form.

You enter your life with a story, a karmic inheritance, and with each life you resolve some karma and carry other karma over with you into the next. We are continually creating karma – our karma, your karma, and the collective karma. It is a deeply enriching continual life's journey over perhaps infinite lifetimes. What better time is there to begin impacting the contents of your karmic suitcase than now?

You Can Live Forever – Genetic Memory

As karma moves through time, from life to life on its journey to being realised, it travels in the etheric body, which you will learn more about in Chapter 6. Not only do we carry through time our karmic messages of our past, we also experience a transfer of information through our genes and through our muscles. Let's look at some examples.

Did you know that if you bisect a flatworm it will grow into two genetically identical worms, like clones? We, of course, don't advise that you try this as an experiment! But it is a fact, that planarian flatworms divide and regenerate indefinitely, and even grow new brains (Gentile et al, 2011). This has been shown in a UK University (Nottingham) where scientists have created a large colony of flatworms all from one original, whose bodies and organs do not appear to age. This shows the steadfast function of gene transference.

When a calf is born to a stock that has been trained not to walk across cattle grids, they won't go near them because they seem to already know the danger of getting trapped. It has become instinctual behaviour held within the genetic makeup of the animal. It allows the animal to engage in an action that it has not been taught before. Similarly, if you place a newborn chick in a large area with a hawk, it will instantly know to run for cover. If you place a newborn chick with a chicken, it will behave as if everything is fine. The chick knows how to react instantly and in a way that is automatic. It's never learned to do that before, it just knows to react in a certain way. These are some examples of a phenomenon where complex abilities and actual knowledge is inherited through genetic memory.

Life experiences, which aren't directly coded in human DNA, can also be passed on. It has been noted that survivors of traumatic events may affect the experiences of subsequent generations. A point in case is the effect that preconception parental trauma has had on the children of Holocaust survivors, who show increased epigenetic alterations, indicating how severe psycho-physiological trauma can have intergenerational effects (Yehuda et al, 2016). This is the nature of genetic memory. So if you have a smell that you hate, ask your grandparents, if you can. Transgenerational genetic inheritance may provide your answers.

Family Constellations therapy, founded by the German psychotherapist Bert Hellinger (1925–), aims to shift destructive familial patterns of suffering that have been 'taken on' through generations within a family. When a child assumes the fate of a parent, the burden can result in anxiety, depression, guilt, aloneness, or illness (for example), absorbed as a means to solidify belonging within the family. Often the presence of a certain member's 'place' within the family is neglected or rejected due to 'abnormal' circumstances. This could be a member of the family being murdered or responsible for abuse or a heinous crime, or a baby being stillborn or aborted. In these cases, Hellinger describes how someone in a later generation is drawn to repeating the rejected family member's fate by sharing a similar misfortune. Through the processes of Family Constellations, it is possible to gain awareness of the pains carried through generations and can lead to what Hellinger describes as the 'Orders of Love' being restored. We (Sandra and Tom) have experienced firsthand the profound depth of this learning, having been part of a powerful Family Constellations process in Romania with incredibly skilled body psychotherapist and facilitator Caterina Farkash, whose story you read about in Chapter 3.

Memory, and karma, is not just passed down through the brain functions and the etheric body, it's passed down through molecules and through genetics, and even muscles. As you may know, your muscles have memory. Have you heard of those people receiving heart transplants taking on the characteristics of the donor? In fact, there have been numerous reports from around the world of organ donors experiencing sudden personality changes and unexpected desires, as well as new intricate skills that they didn't possess before their organ transplant.

In her book *Love in the Blood* (2014), French actress Charlotte Valandrey wrote about the impact on her in the months following her heart transplant. She began to experience recurring nightmares of being in a car crash in which she was blinded by oncoming headlights in the rain. She also described how her tastes had completely changed, such as a new-found liking for wine, which she had never enjoyed previously. Charlotte was insistent that these feelings and memories were those of her donor.

After two kidney transplants, thirty-seven-year-old Cheryl Johnson, of Preston, England, claims that with each kidney came a drastic change in her personality. After the first transplant, she reported suddenly becoming 'stroppy and snappy', which was unlike her general demeanour. After the second transplant, she developed a short temper, along with a sudden craving for classic literature, including Jane Austen and Fyodor Dostoyevsky. This was in sharp contrast to her old reading habits.

Jamie Sherman, from Tucson, Arizona, received her heart transplant at the age of twenty-four. On awakening from the procedure, she felt a deep sense of unexplained anger to the degree that she wanted to get up and fight. She had also developed a new craving for Mexican food and cheese enchiladas in particular. When she finally met the family of her donor, a man named Scott, she discovered that Scott's favourite food was Mexican and especially cheese enchiladas! More to her surprise, she also discovered that Scott had died in an angry altercation at a sports bar and believed that these feelings were locked in his heart when it was transplanted in her.

THE COLLECTIVE UNCONSCIOUS

In exploring what influences our lives, we can also look to the concept of the 'collective unconscious'. Jung believed that the collective unconscious was an accumulation of knowledge and images that every human being possesses from birth, inherited from prior generations of humans. We may think of the collective unconscious as a body of wisdom passed down from our ancestors, inherited by us all. Although you personally are unaware of what is contained in the collective unconscious, in times of crisis your psyche may open a door to the symbolic collective unconscious in order to allow personal growth to occur. This usually happens via dreams, where understanding can be gained from their symbolic representations. Usually those dreams are so 'way out' that they are beyond your normal 'processing' dream function. Jung noted that certain dream symbols possess the same universal messages for all men and women, and that a true exploration of the various meanings they offer through their symbolic representations can lead to deep insight.

These symbols and images, ever-present in the collective unconscious, are described in Jungian theory as archetypes, primitive mental images inherited from our earliest human ancestors (Jung, 2004). These include your 'shadow', the repressed aspects of yourself that are often portrayed as a murderer, a bully, or pursuer. To bring this idea alive in your mind, think of Robert Louis Stevenson's story *Dr Jekyll and Mr Hyde*.

Dr Henry Jekyll, a man of great medical stature, spends a significant part of his life attempting to suppress the apparent evil urges he dreads succumbing to, that unleashed, would paint him in a terrible light to all his contemporaries. He concocts a special serum that once ingested, represses and thus hides this evil within his personality. However, in doing so, Jekyll unintentionally unleashes his shadow, the deep, dark, hidden depths of his disowned self –

Mr Edward Hyde, a hideous, evil, and dangerous creature who holds neither compassion nor remorse for his actions. You might connect to your shadow side when you suddenly act out of character, when you have an intense dislike of somebody, or through your dreams.

Your dreams may unearth not only your shadow but other paradoxical aspects of your personality. These could include the *Anima* and *Animus*, the female and male characteristics that we all possess. Expression of these archetypes illuminates an appreciation of the essential facets of these characteristics, and where there is a need for greater balance. These might appear in dreams as highly feminine or masculine figures, asking you to open yourself up to more of your feminine or masculine qualities. You might also uncover the *Divine Child*, the epitome of your true self, usually represented in dreams by a baby or young child that symbolises your innocence and carries an innate sense of vulnerability. Here you may be shown the child to connect with your aspirations and to remind you to strive towards your full potential. In connecting with this aspect of yourself through your dreams, you are being challenged to connect more with the authentic you rather than the persona you've created for the world you live in. Other archetypes shown to you could be the *Wise Old Woman* or *Man*, symbolizing the helper; the *Great Mother* as the nurturer; the *Trickster*, helping you not take yourself too seriously; and the *Persona*, your public mask. And there are many more.

The collective unconscious refers to a segment of the deepest unconscious mind not shaped by personal experience. It is innately inherited and common to all human beings. As an example, it has been found that one-third of British children at six years old are afraid of snakes, even though it's very rare to encounter a snake in a traumatic situation, especially in the UK. Nevertheless, snakes still generated an anxious response (Jones, 2000). Also, if you introduce children between the ages of one to five to a rabbit and a snake, they are likely to be curious about the rabbit and have a degree of fear for the snake. This suggests that a fear of snakes is located in the collective unconscious.

At this point, we have explored the notions of karma, genetic memory, and the collective unconscious. Perhaps this is a good time for you to recap in your workbook some of your thoughts and feelings that came as you were reading about these ideas.

Jung, as he was nearing the end of his life, wrote, "I could well imagine that I might have lived in former centuries and there encountered questions I was not yet able to answer; that I had been born again because I had not fulfilled the task given to me" (cited in Lucas, 2008, p. 318–319). We wonder where he is now and what work he is looking to fulfil.

We've covered a lot in this chapter. We started with getting you to think about the notion of unfinished business and what open loops you may have been carrying in your life, which we hope you'll be able to continue working at closing. We've also looked at the fascinating subject of time, which is such a crucial aspect of connecting to past life therapy, as moving through time and considering the idea of a parallel universe is what enables you to open up to the process of this work fully. We hope that by also considering your karma, and what you inherit through genetic memory and the collective unconscious, you recognise the vastness of what is within you in your current existence.

Exploring all of this shows the complexities of being human, moving as a vessel of messages and learnings through eternal time.

In Chapter 1 we looked at the common question posed by so many people . . . "There *must* be more to life than this, mustn't there?" We sincerely hope now that you're able to explore this with a new level of confidence! Let's move to the next chapter then and get even closer to who you are and what you carry within.

Chapter 5
It's Nice to Meet Me!

He who knows others is wise;
he who knows himself is enlightened.
Lao Tzu

Connecting to More of You

Up until this chapter we have asked you to reflect upon and describe your thoughts and feelings, your experience of the higher-self and soul visualisation, as well as what you see as your open loops and other small exercises such as the two-minute challenge. We hope you have managed to make some notes either in the workbook or in your own journal.

In this chapter, we will be asking further questions in order to get you more connected to yourself; who you are, and how you have been living. It is important in starting a process of self-exploration such as you are doing within this book, to begin from knowing more about yourself in your current life. In becoming more aware of what's behind the choices you make and the images you hold of yourself in your life, you discover and uncover questions in need of answering. In exploring your past lives you can find answers to these questions and also find answers to questions that have yet to surface into your conscious mind, but are nevertheless there, just out of reach at this moment in time.

AGNES

In one of our Past Life Transpersonal Therapy courses, unearthing more about herself led Agnes, a course participant, to finding some answers she had been looking for. She wondered why she struggled so much with her outer life (reality), which was different to her inner life (which she called home). It was like she was in a constant battle with herself as she strove for acceptance from others, whilst at the same time finding herself doing things that she knew people would disapprove of. She always put so much energy into everything she tried to do and yet she felt this was never good enough for others and to some extent herself. She was exhausted because of how hard she worked and was frustrated and sad because she always felt a failure and lacked a sense of belonging.

In her past life session, Agnes went back to age twenty in the 1920's, finding herself in a room, having been dragged there by her hair. She was being treated very badly by her husband who was a bar owner, and who expected her to entertain his drunken clientele. As she was dragged away that day, all in the bar were jeering and laughing at her. She was then locked in a room as a punishment and left there, as she often was, for days on end. In moving forward in time in that past life, she became aware of experiencing a tremendously hard life serving others and had surrendered to what she believed to be her fate of abuse and punishment. There were no hopes or dreams of escaping her life of squalor and all she really wanted to do was just die.

In moving her forward in time again, she found herself thrown into a sewer and abandoned. When taking her to the last day of her young life, all she wanted was for her life to end so she could be free. It was such a short and abusive life with no chance to be herself. She was totally restricted and confined to do as she was bid, and so leaving her life, dying and moving out of her body was a huge relief.

As the past life session came to an end and we moved to exploring what she had learned from the process she became very emotional. She recognised that in her current life, she had been a very strong rebel, awkward at times in fact. She realised that she was holding a feeling of never wanting to be trapped, and now she knew why. She was *never* ending up abused and in that sewer again, discarded and left to die.

The session gave her the understanding of why she was always trying to be a rebel and yet at the same time trying to fit in. This was the beginning of giving herself permission to be herself. She recognised why she continually struggled to do the things she wanted to do and why she constantly considered other people's opinions above her own, hence her outer and inner worlds never matched.

A month after the session, I (Sandra) asked her how she had been and what the longer-term impact of our session was. She told me that she had become aware of the submissive energy that she had been living with and how this had stopped her choosing more of what she wanted in her life. Agnes now feels so much more comfortable to follow her own dreams and to be herself. The connections she made from her past life experiences with her current life way of being were powerfully life changing. She has answers to her questions and thus has been able to connect to more of herself.

The Power of Writing

Let's start now to get you more connected to yourself. You can make the most of this chapter by referring to your workbook and completing the exercises as we go along. It's possible to discover a great deal through engaging in reflecting and writing about yourself. Writing things down brings you into the state of mindfulness and calls you to attend to yourself. It engages many parts of the brain as you explore what you think and feel, formulate these into words, and then externalise your insights by writing them down. It helps you unravel your inner truth, offering you deeper insight into knowing how you really feel, and in the process of expressing this you enhance your mental health and wellbeing.

The enhancement of your self-awareness offers you a route to healing – emotionally, physically, and psychologically. Writing in this way has been found to improve immune functions, lower your blood pressure and lift your mood (Matousek, 2017; Pennebaker, 2004).

It's helpful to take a few moments to ponder on each of the questions and go beyond your first initial thought, as this will take you to greater depths within yourself. So, for example, the first main question asks you to consider if you are a leader, rebel, hero, coward, or rescuer. Our advice is to think instantly which one you are drawn to and then go through each one and become aware of your reactions to them. Then you can engage more intimately with yourself and get closer to your truth.

Let's do a 'warm up' exercise to begin freely and creatively imagining. Write down your thoughts, feelings, and the images that come into your mind for the following words. Let what comes to you from within flow freely in your mind unquestioned.

- Mountains.
- Celebrations.
- The colour red.
- Snow.
- Tunnels.
- A dog barking.
- A child crying.
- Stroking an animal.
- The feel of a fire.
- A cold crisp morning.

What have you noticed as you completed this? Are there any patterns you can see?

It's important to remember that at this stage, any strong emotional images or reactions may come from your past lives, so make a note of when this happens.

Let's take this further. Write something about yourself now regarding your tastes in the following areas.

- Home and furnishings.
- Clothes.
- Food and eating.
- Music.
- Books and movies.
- Interests and hobbies.

As you begin to get the creative part of your mind engaged, let's see how we can connect this to your past lives.

Crossing Your Mind

Let's further consider your present life and explore potential clues that can be indicators of the content of some of your past lives. What can you already find out about them based on your current thoughts, feelings, desires, and passions? Make one or two choices from each of the nine questions below that apply to you and circle them. This can give you a solid base from where to begin your past life exploration.

1. **Do you consider yourself a ...**
   Leader,
   Rebel,
   Hero,

Coward,
Rescuer,
Creator,
Something else?

2. **What do you most relate to?**

A vivid imagination.
A strong hold on reality.
Idealism.
A need to help and protect others.
A spiritual connection to the world.

3. **In a heated discussion . . .**

I stick to my guns.
I look for common ground.
I try everything to convince the other.
I just want to sound right.
I back down.
I agree with their argument.
I avoid at all costs anything contentious.
Something else?

4. **Which appeals to you most?**

Fantasy.
Action.
Mystery.
Romance.
Art and poetry.
Academia.
Science.
Business.
Something else?

5. **How would you positively describe yourself?**

Spontaneous.
Energetic.

Friendly.
Life and soul of the party.
Free thinking.
Popular.
Comedian/entertainer.
Something else?

6. **How would you negatively describe yourself?**
Boring.
Arrogant.
Overly sensitive.
Hot tempered.
Lazy.
Crazy.
Disorganized.
Something else?

7. **What do you value the most?**
Family and friends.
Happiness.
Money.
Being productive.
Being highly thought of.
Being in control.
Something else?

8. **Do you prefer . . .**
Libraries,
Churches,
Historical buildings,
The countryside,
Cities/towns,
Something else?

9. **Do you like . . .**
Reading,

Writing,
Drawing,
Watching entertainment,
Walking,
Socialising,
Something else?

- How do these relate to any struggles you have in your life now?
- What do these descriptions of yourself lead you to consider when thinking about your past lives and unfinished business?

WHO WERE YOU?

We are now going to focus on places and countries you are drawn to, as well as eras you have an affinity with and things you love to do.

TRAVEL AND PLACES

The White Mountain Apache Tribe, located in the east central region of Arizona, USA, place a great importance on spaces. Indeed, the Apache traditions relating to the passing down of history doesn't attach events to specific chronological dates, as do western traditions. Instead, they tell history through geographical space and by naming places. They say that wisdom sits in certain places and that when talking of these places they are able to access not only the story that goes with them but also the ethic that informs how one should live (Raffensperger, 2012).

Think for a moment about the place that you live and the places that you have lived in and travelled to. Consider how you came to be in that place. If you would or could move away to another place, where would that be? Also, where would you definitely not want to be? Have you been somewhere that you have felt really at home in, loving the people, the food, the music and the culture? What wisdom, history, and messages have those places carried for you?

Begin to ponder upon where you are drawn to going in the future. Is there any part of the world that you long to go to? There doesn't have to be any particular reason. It may be simply a yearning.

There have been lots of places we (Sandra and Tom) have needed to go in the world and places in the world that we really feel at home in – as well as some places that we don't. There is no rhyme or reason to this, it just is. There are also places we would like to visit just to see how we feel in them and other parts of the world that we are curious about. In our past lives we most definitely connect to travel as a big part of who we were, because something most definitely draws us both to travelling.

When Tom gets to an airport, he feels at home and alive – the smell of aviation fuel, the check-in bustle, getting on the plane . . . he loves flying and traveling and visiting different countries. Sandra also loves to travel. The moment she arrives at the airport there is not only a sense of freedom but also of feeling at home and with a greater sense of clarity. When we are travelling we are both at our most creative. Each kind of journey has its own qualities: sun or ski holidays are very different from trips to delivering presentations and workshops, and from those times when we are drawn to visiting a particular location, such as our very moving trip to Auschwitz, which fulfilled a long-held desire. What touches us deeply is that no matter where we are in the world, what excites us is sitting in a café surrounded by the locals, reflecting and talking nonstop philosophy. We come alive in a way that is incredibly invigorating. We laugh and joke that perhaps we were Jean-Paul Sartre and Simone De Beauvoir in our past lives. Having read about them and their lives, they loved to do that too.

Think about this in relation to yourself. Do you like to travel or stay at home? Are there places that you want to experience and places that you definitely don't want to go to? Are there places that you have been and loved, and places that you have hated? This might even be in the country that you live in now or maybe another land.

Take some time to think about the world and where you live in it and what all this might mean. Make a few notes so you have a record of your thoughts:

ERAS

Now let's move on to thinking about historical eras that fascinate you. Are you drawn towards the 1930's? Or do you study a great deal the Victorian times, or other eras from the distant past? Think beyond what historical periods you were taught at school or college and look at what era you simply feel drawn to. Perhaps look at some of the knick-knacks that you have collected over the years. Is there a particular style and era that they have come from? Tom tends to have a lot of the First and Second World War items around him that he has collected or been given. Sandra is fascinated by ancient Egyptian times and has gathered quite a few artefacts from this era. Do you feel you were born in the wrong era, with a sense you would have been much more comfortable in the Georgian times because you can really relate to Jane Austin's novels or the clothing or jewellery relevant to that period? Make a few notes again of your thoughts:

PEOPLE

Now let's move on to the type of people that you are drawn to. Do you like to read certain types of books about certain types of people? Are there specific types of people that you enjoy being around? Have you had dealings with particular types of people more than others? Are there people that have had a profound effect on you and your life?

There might be people that you've come across and thought, "I've definitely met you before", even though you know that you haven't. Maybe there is someone that you simply 'get' and who also gets you, without you having had years of friendship to know each other. What type of person are they? Make a few notes of your thoughts:

Talents

What are you able to do that has always come naturally to you, without any effort at all? What talents do you feel you were born with? What talents were, for you, easy to cultivate or easy to pick up, like you just knew how to do it right from the beginning? Continue to record your thoughts:

Déjà Vu

Have you ever experienced déjà vu? Like you've been somewhere in a previous time, and it just hits you — boom — "I've been here before." In truth you haven't, yet you *know* you have. Write down your thoughts:

All of the information you have gleaned throughout this chapter will help you on the next part of the journey.

You have thought about many aspects of yourself in this chapter, so it's important now to begin to step back and notice any gaps in what you have written. Let's summarise and bring this all together.

Write a couple of pages in your workbook on the following:

1. What would your closest friends and family be most surprised to learn about from what you have written in this chapter?

By finding these words you are going deeper inside yourself, exploring the roots of your earliest beliefs and identity and where you might have been born into in your past lives.

2. Describe some of what you have written in this chapter that you feel is problematic or disempowering in this life.

3. How much of yourself do you keep hidden? Have you denied yourself honest answers in this chapter? Just consider for a moment if you could have written something different.

4. Using your imagination . . . where or what might you have been in a previous life. Let your imagination go wild and see where it takes you. Write several scenarios that come to mind for you.

In this chapter we have encouraged you to think about your present life from a variety of different perspectives. We wonder how you have felt and what has occurred in these exercises. Awakening is an ongoing experience and something to continue mindfully.

One final exploration . . . what role in life would you most love to play? What do you most deeply want? If there were no barriers, no financial implications . . . what would you be doing in your life right now? Exploring in this way helps you navigate your inner world, and your words can help you understand what is blocking your way. So, keep writing.

Now you are ready to continue your journey into the deeper essence of your past lives.

CHAPTER 6
EXPANDING POSSIBILITIES

Within each of us is a light, awake,
encoded in the fibers of our existence.
Tony Samara

QUANTUM PHYSICS

Let's step briefly into the world of physics and physiology. Here we can observe ourselves as simply vibrational 'beings', radiating our own unique energy, affecting and impacting the world around us.

Your brain, in all its complexity – much of which we have yet to gain understanding of – is made up of a network of nerve cells, all interacting with each other and generating electrical activity (Callaway, 1975). So as you read this book and the words on this page, your mind is processing this information. What you are thinking about are all degrees of electrical impulses that can be measured. Not only your brain, but your entire body has an electrical field. Any time you've felt the shock of static electricity as you touch someone or something, or used a touch-sensitive screen, your electric field is at work. So we are more than just our thoughts and what we do; we are energy – living vibrations that impact the world.

Quantum physics offers fascinating new insights about the world we live in. As Yusim (2017) writes, "According to quantum physics, at a level of reality that is invisible to the human eye, everything and everybody is interconnected with one another and to all living organisms" (p. xxxiii).

Do you know of the book and movie *The Secret* by Rhonda Byrne (2006)? This worldwide, popular phenomenon put forward the notion that we can attract things to us purposely through the practice of visualisation, gratitude, and intention. Now, whether you accept the message in *The Secret* that just by thinking about something you can attract it, or not, there is no denying that we can influence the world and people around us. The physiological energetic states we are all in and our focus of attention, impact our experiences, and by becoming more aware of these we can be more alive and responsive to our surroundings.

For example, if all of us are in a peaceful, loving state inside, it will inevitably impact the external world around us and influence how others feel as well. Have you ever been around a happy and contented group of people or been around someone who is very down and melancholy? Has some of their energy rubbed off on you? Of course! What *The Secret*, and other popular books that followed, such as Glenn Harrold's *The Answer* (2011), did was to open people's awareness to the idea that there's more than just what we see, what we hear, and what we feel. They challenged people to consider thinking differently about their life, what was in it, what wasn't, and why.

There's so much more to the world and so much more to be discovered within the notions of time and energy than many people realise or even consider. This is because what we understand and believe about these things and about concepts such as the universe have been gleaned from our learnings, thus are essentially mental constructions – ideas or theories. R.C. Henry (2005), Professor of Physics and Astronomy at Johns Hopkins University, writes,

> A fundamental conclusion of the new (quantum) physics also acknowledges that the observer creates the reality. As observers, we are personally involved with the creation of our own reality. Physicists are being forced to admit that the universe is a 'mental' construction. (p. 29)

We wanted to open your mind to viewing time and energy outside of the traditional norms that we are encouraged to live within. The notion of past lives is certainly outside of many peoples' normal everyday awareness, as is quantum physics. However, transcending the 'norm' can help expand your ability to realise your potential as you challenge yourself to see life at a more diverse and deeper level, beyond what is influenced by your constructed thoughts. Think of all the energy you are putting out there; think of yourself as a being of energy and vibration, influencing the energy and vibrations in and around the world, the universe, other people, indeed all living things and even material objects. How does it feel to consider the magnitude of your vibes?

Akashic Records

The concept of the energy of 'being' also introduces the ideas of the Akashic records and the etheric body.

> The Akashic Records are a dimension of consciousness that contains a vibrational record of every soul and its journey. As such, the Records are an experiential body of knowledge that contains everything that every soul has ever thought, said, and done over the course of its existence, as well as all its future possibilities. (Howe, 2009, p. 4)

Put simply, the Akashic records refers to a database of every word, thought, or action that is stored energetically and encoded in a non-physical plane of existence. In this way, each of us is connected to one another. "It is the unending expanse of vibrating consciousness that is both our shared and individual truth" (Taylor, 2016, p. 3).

Your records leads you to all that has become your present and can help reveal your potential future based on your present energy and direction (which is not yet written in stone). Woolger (2010) describes how the notion of the Akashic records are viewed in differing ways: "The scholar Joseph Campbell called it mythical reality. The aborigines in Australia call it the dreamtime" (p. 20).

Akasha is the Sanskrit word for sky, space, ether, or atmosphere. Your Akashic records are the records of your soul's journey in which are held all your thoughts, feelings, actions, and deeds – from each lifetime. You could imagine the Akashic record as a library with each book representing a lifetime(s) of everyone and everything, or perhaps you could look at it as everyone's life stored in the hard drive of a universal computer. They are akin to a universal filing system, storing all the magnetic vibrations of everything out in the ether. As these records are accessed through being in a deep state of relaxation or meditation, anyone can have access to the Akashic records. They are timeless, comprehensive, and accessible. When you have flashes of intuition or a hunch, you are accessing the records. When you guide your dreams or work on esoteric exercises you can access the records – your records.

The Akashic records were written about extensively in the nineteenth century, in particular by Edgar Cayce (1877–1945). He found that he had intuitive abilities when he took himself into a meditative state where he was able to place his mind in contact with all time and space – the universal consciousness. From there he could respond to a variety of questions, accessing answers to medical issues and healing advice that would successfully help people. All in all, he used the Akashic records to do nearly two thousand readings of past lives as well as helping medical diagnosis and healing, and to make future predictions for people. He had all these recorded, aware that he got his information from the individual's unconscious mind and the Akashic records.

The most important stance here is to be fully open and ready, because a reading into your Akashic records is to awaken to the power of your soul, to discover your purest voice, and to change your future. Through this process we can identify what past traumas and blocks are within you that have left an energetic imprint and are impacting your present life. In this we see how you align with your karmic message. This is empowering, as not only do you have the ability to gather the information you need, you also have the ability to change your records and transform present patterns to bring the resolution you are looking for.

> All of our outcomes exist in energetic potential and even the slightest change that we make now can create dramatically divergent results in our destiny. The ultimate solution is to reclaim our power, determining what we write in every present future. (Taylor, 2016, Loc. 214)

When accessing your Akashic records, you're also needing to access your higher self. Remember this is the highest aspect of you that can be realised, your 'I Am' presence. It is the part of you that is vibrating at a higher frequency than your physical self, and that knows and understands at the highest possible level, sensing more about what you need than you do. It is your higher self that you will need to connect with so that you can reach within, at the soul level, and begin to get to know what is in your records. It can be enlightening to connect regularly with the records, which you can revisit as often as you want.

So where are the Akashic records? They are within the ether all around you. Think in terms of all human beings and any other life form as having an etheric body, that occupies the same space as the physical body but extends beyond the surface of the skin. The human etheric body is the vibrating network of energy from which our energetic blueprint is created and is important for our wellbeing. The energy increases and decreases depending upon your emotions and thoughts, and it functions at the same frequency as the ether. Its strength and vitality can be undermined by events and behaviours such as shock, trauma, and drug and alcohol use, as well as being affected by unresolved issues and unfinished business. We are out in the ether and impacting the world in more ways than we know.

Your personal records hold the details of every experience in every lifetime you have ever lived. Through these you form habits, patterns, and attachments that all get written in the record of your eternal life. Karma is the workings of the cause and effect that becomes part of your records. As you access and explore the records through PLTT you gain greater knowledge about issues that you are dealing with now – the repeated behaviours, thoughts, and feelings that speak your karmic message – and become empowered to rewrite patterns so you can move in a new direction.

When you think about something you would like to happen, you are sending that thought as a vibration out into the ether. This changes the ether, where thought is reality. That is why so often what you think about tends to materialise – because the energy around you has changed and a new reality is created. So if you are thinking about bad things always happening to you and sending that out into the ether via your thoughts and statements, the energy around you will be exactly that – you are opening yourself up to attracting bad things. If you think about something that you really want, then that too sends out those vibrations. It's therefore not just what we do in life that determines what we get, it's who we are, what we believe in, how we think and communicate our thoughts, as well as who we imagine we will become that influences our experiences. It is all about energy. *All* of this goes out into the ether. The legendary thinker and inventor Nikola Tesla wrote way back in 1907, in his unpublished paper *Man's Greatest Achievement*:

> All perceptible matter comes from a primary substance, or tenuity beyond conception, filling all space, the akasha or luminiferous ether, which is acted upon by the life giving Prana or creative force, calling into existence, in never-ending cycles all things and phenomena.

Let's look at this in a practical way for a moment. Have you ever travelled somewhere inside your mind and thought about and imagined somebody? Indeed, you might even do that now, and let your mind drift to a particular person. When you think of that person, notice where you think of them being, their surroundings, how they are going about their business, and doing their thing. In doing this you've actually travelled there in your mind, wondering, looking at, and watching what they're doing and how they're being. Strangely, the person that you were thinking about often connects with you in some way. This is because those thoughts of yours are vibrations out in the ether which reach their vibrations. Synchronicity in action.

Sandra recently experienced this connection. She was thinking about someone she had known when she was a teacher, twenty-odd years ago, wondering what had happened to her and imagining what she was doing right now. Lo and behold that same afternoon, that very person popped up in a Facebook messenger post and said, "Hello! How are you?" and they started to catch up on the intervening years. That's more than a coincidence, isn't it? That thought, Sandra's imagining, was in the ether and her friend, not spoken to in over twenty years, was able to pick up on it, experience it, and react to it. How many times has that happened to you?

Through exploring the Akashic records and your past lives, you can alter the past, present, and future, causing a shift that can adjust the power and energy of your present life and thus your future. You become less burdened with the past, as you close the unfinished business and thus shift the energy of your consciousness towards being genuinely present in the now. Since all time is vibrating at the same time, changing your records releases you from past events and their influence over you. This opens you to a greater sense of personal and spiritual power which your soul embraces, continuing to look for higher vibrations to live more consciously, connected, and enlightened.

Consider for a moment the Akashic records having a view of all the future potential that is yours. Its vitality and flow means that it has the ability to store what is most likely to happen to you based on your energy now and your present day actions. It makes sense that if you don't become more enlightened as to your potential, then you will continue to repeat your patterns. Choosing that same partner who always turns out to change significantly once you moved in together, that job that somehow ends up with you getting bullied or sidelined in promotions, or any other pattern that is energetically created by you, as if stuck on auto-loop.

Let's begin to make a difference then. Here is an exercise to begin programming future Akashic records for yourself.

1. Imagine your most successful self. How do you really want to be, feel, and act? Let's raise your vibrations. Record how you would be, feel, and act in various situations as your most successful and empowered self.

- In work situations.
- In social situations.
- In intimate relationships.

Begin to consider the goals that you really desire in your life, exactly as you want them to be. Write a short one-page story about this:

There are further specific exercises that you can do to open yourself up more to accessing the Akashic records. The following can help you to raise your vibrations and a higher state of consciousness that achieves a wider and deeper openness to your life experience, and thus the Akashic records. You'll find out more about raising your vibrations in the next few paragraphs.

In the meantime, engaging in the following exercises can make a big difference:

2. Meditate regularly. Imagine, as you breathe deeply, travelling in your mind for a few minutes to a place you find incredibly peaceful, tranquil, and inspiring.

3. Deep breathing. Every two to three hours practice deep breathing from your stomach. Inhale for the count of four – allowing your stomach to fully expand – hold for seven and exhale for eight. This helps oxygenate your body to mentally and physically relax.
4. Become 'hearty'. Move your attention to your heart as much as you can. Imagine a light emanating from your heart and filling your body with powerful and healing vibrations.
5. Take it a step further: Imagine your 'heart-energy' reaching out and touching another heart in the world. Who would it be? What would the message of the energy be?

The Akashic records hold an immense storehouse of information, as well as a wealth of potential. We don't think we can conclude the Akashic records in any better way than Taylor's (2016) words:

> The greatest Akashic Cause is to live in the heart of purpose and appreciation, to be ever conscious of your soul's intentions and ever grateful for each precious moment that is your life's expression. The work that you do, the healing that you seek, the peace and joy that you long for – engaging in all of this with courage and perseverance is a causal choice that resonates with life itself. And the Akashic Effect is a life of profound connections and miraculous occurrences just waiting to come your way. (p. 185)

Raising Your Vibrations

Let's look further at the vibration level you need to reach to be able to connect with yourself at a more profound level in general, where accessing your Akashic records is possible. It is likely that you'll need to raise your vibrations to a much higher frequency. We've just explored four ways to begin to do this above, but let's look at what else you can do.

How can you continue to raise your frequency? To start with, you can look to show courage, find acceptance, and work on experiencing happiness, joy, gratitude, and love as much as possible.

All of these things raise your vibrations, and the higher your vibrations, the higher your consciousness. The higher your consciousness, the more you can access.

Whatever you are experiencing in life at the moment, there is always room for this. Might it feel hard to do? Yes. Is it worthwhile? Definitely. So, you might show courage by finally taking on an aspect of your life that you've been avoiding because fear has stopped you. You could commit to accepting a situation that you cannot change and let go, reclaiming the energy that was being drained from you by fighting against it. You might look at your life and find just one thing that brings you happiness, no matter how small it is, and do this regularly. How could you accentuate that and allow it to bring you joy? Also, what in your life can you be thankful for? What can you show genuine gratitude for, and how can you expand that to feel love?

To formulate how you can begin to raise your vibrations, write in your workbook some of the things that you can do to:

- Show courage.
- Find acceptance.
- Experience happiness and joy.
- Experience gratitude and love.

Brain States and Consciousness

Let's explore now the various levels of consciousness so that you can fully understand the levels you need to practice accessing. Then, you will be able to reach and draw from them for a past life therapy healing session and generally experience a more expansive and fulfilling life.

Brain waves are produced by synchronized electrical pulses from neurons (nerve cells) communicating with each other. Our thoughts, emotions, and behaviours are the communication of these neurons and are thus electrical impulses. Our brain waves change according to what we are doing, thinking, and how we are feeling. When slower brain waves dominate . . . we are left feeling tired or dreamy, whilst faster brain waves leave us feeling wired or hyper-alert.

Here we describe a summary of the various brain states, showing how the lowering of frequencies impact states of consciousness. We'll also explore the states of consciousness where past life therapy takes place. For each of the brain states we describe what can happen if there is too much or too little activity. However, as we human beings are complex and multi-layered, individually we will respond differently in relation to the brain state activity. Some people might, for example, experience anxiety, whilst others experience depression.

Brain State	Frequency	State of Consciousness
Gamma	Typically around 40Hz	**The Unity State** Gamma waves can link information from all parts of the brain and are associated with bursts of insight, high-level information processing, and cognitive functioning (learning and memory). Gamma waves bind all our senses in regard to perception and are involved in learning new material. They are associated with **expanded awareness** and characteristically experienced by regular meditators (see Fell et al., 2010). Described as creating 'feelings of blessings' by experienced meditators, gamma brainwave activity, if too much, can cause anxiety and stress; if too little, depression, learning difficulties, and conditions such as ADHD.

Beta	14–40Hz	**The Conscious Realm** Fully awake and alert. Generally associated with normal waking consciousness and active for effective functioning through the day at tasks such as critical thinking, reading, writing, socialisation, left-brain thinking activity, logic, and critical reasoning. Also prone to tuning into nagging doubts and self-criticism, potentially leading to stress and anxiety. Substances that increase beta waves include various stimulants such as coffee and caffeinated energy drinks.
Alpha	8–13Hz	**The Subconscious Gateway** Alpha is the gateway to your subconscious mind, at the base of your conscious awareness. It bridges the gap between your conscious thinking and the subconscious mind. Here you'll be relaxing, daydreaming, and in light meditation. Alpha brain waves are generally associated with right-brain creative thinking activity – a key state for relaxation and programming your mind for success. Alpha brain waves heighten your imagination, visualisation, memory, learning, and concentration. During times of stress, a phenomenon called 'alpha blocking' may occur, resulting in excessive beta activity and very little alpha. This can also lead to insomnia and OCD. Alcohol, marijuana, and some antidepressants increase alpha waves.

<table>
<tr><td colspan="2">Theta 4–8Hz

The gateway to Past Life Therapy work</td><td>The Subconscious Realm

Deeply relaxed, daydreaming, and restorative sleep, with access to insights and deep and raw emotions. Your mind's most deep-rooted programs are at theta frequency, where you experience bursts of creativity, vivid visualisations, intuitive ideas, and deep insight.

This is the realm of your subconscious that you experience as you drift into sleep from alpha and awaken from deep sleep (delta).

Theta is a key state for 'reality' creation through vivid imagery and for entering past lives, where you can experience deep spiritual connection and unity with the universe. It is the optimal state for visualisation and mind programming as it is where you consciously create your reality.

Too much theta activity can make people susceptible to experiences of depression, hyperactivity, and impulsivity. Too little can lead to anxiety, reduced emotional awareness, and stress. At this frequency, you can become highly suggestible, due to being in a hypnotic trance state.</td></tr>
<tr><td>Delta</td><td>0.5– 3.5Hz</td><td>The Unconscious Realm

Dreamless. Generally associated with no thinking. Here there is access to non-physical states of existence. Delta provides a key state for healing, regeneration, and rejuvenation. It is also involved in unconscious bodily functions such as regulating your heart beat and digestion.</td></tr>
</table>

		Delta is the slowest recorded frequency in human beings and is experienced in deep sleep as well as deep transcendental meditation. Delta waves are most often found in infants and young children. Delta state is the gateway to the **universal and collective unconscious**.

In summary, our brain and consciousness are inextricably linked, meaning our brainwave patterns influence our experience of consciousness. In raising our vibrational levels, we raise our brain waves, to gamma state, which enhances our state of well-being, awareness and creativity. It heightens our intuition and mental clarity, enabling access to deep feelings of peace, joy, and oneness.

In lowering our brain waves to theta state, we are also able to connect with creativity and inspiration, and access the ability for vivid visualisations. Clearly there are profound benefits to altering our brain waves into these two states. This allows your consciousness, and awareness, different 'lenses' of perspective, fostering an expansive and richly healing experience, where you become open to deep learning in relation to your Akashic records and karmic grooves.

Let's move now onto Part 2 of the book, where we begin to move into the experience and process of Past Life Transpersonal Therapy.

Healing From The Other Side

~ Part Two ~

'Knowing is not enough; we must apply.'
~ Leonardo da Vinci ~

~ **PART TWO** ~

CHAPTER 7

CAST YOUR MIND BACK

Home's where you go when you run out of homes.
John le Carré, *The Honourable Schoolboy*

THE MECHANICS

As we mentioned in the introduction chapter, this book can be used by both therapists and those wishing to find out how past life therapy can work for them personally. This next section will help you from either of these perspectives to understand the mechanics of how hypnotic trance is used to facilitate the past life exploration.

When looking at brain waves, and levels of consciousness, we find that in hypnosis two very important things happen:

1. The brain's frequency slows down to the same rate as it was running at up to the age of roughly six years – theta state. This is a prime state for learning things rapidly.

2. The conscious critical faculty, which acts as a filter of the mind's activity, is dampened down. This is the part that analyses, solves problems, makes decisions, and is critical of the content that it is processing. It's that chatter inside your mind. Without this conscious critical factor in full flow, you can feel less self-conscious, with a lessened connection to your rational and logical consideration, and more open and able to connect with yourself and your past selves.

Leading authority in children's intuitive development Elly Molina (2017) describes the transformational potential of this brain state:

> During theta, children remain highly impressionable. Like sponges, they absorb everything around them from their parents, caregivers, teachers, books, TV shows, and firsthand experiences. Filters for judgment or discernment have not yet developed, so this information gets stored and embedded in the subconscious mind. Theta connects us to the world of imagination, creation, fantasy, even a certain kind of 'knowingness' and 'oneness', . . . with little or no critical, rational thinking or judgement. (p. 26)

In Your Own Time – The Hypnotic Induction

For Past Life Transpersonal Therapy, we want to work from within the theta state. Therefore, we need to be able to guide someone into this state so that the therapeutic work can be successfully undertaken.

To do this, we use a step-by-step approach that carefully creates a hypnotic trance state through physical bodily relaxation, mental relaxation, and the use of suggestions about past lives. Time distortion is also utilised within the regression back into the past life experience. It will be rare for someone not to go somewhere within their past lives after a process like this as these methods include some of the most powerful hypnotic trance inducing processes we know.

If you are new to this and don't already have some knowledge of hypnosis and an awareness of the basic inductions and hypnotic language patterns, then take a look at *The Hypnosis Resource Hub* (see the resources section at the end of the book). You can also learn more in Roy Hunter's *The Art of Hypnosis* (2010), or Rubin Battino and Thomas South's *Ericksonian Approaches* (2005). These books will guide you through some of the basics.

Here is a breakdown of the first part of the process in which hypnotic trance is utilised for the regression:

1. **Settling down and preparation for induction** by using generalizations, truisms, common experiences, and yes-sets, to prepare the client for the past life discovery.

2. **Physical bodily relaxation** via classical passive progressive relaxation. Taking each part of the body and the experience of relaxing the muscles in that area and combining this with embedded regression suggestions. The hypnotic induction is most powerful if you include this physical relaxation as it allows for non-direct suggestion, which is more permeative than direct commands.

3. **Mind relaxation** – By using confusion techniques and ambiguous language, we begin to make our words non-logical so that they grab the creative attention of the mind, which then tries to make continual sense of what is being said. This increases confusion – a powerful hypnotic trance deepener. Focusing attention is a key component of hypnosis. As the delta state is too deep to do much of the work needed in past life therapy (whilst providing us with the deep connection necessary from the universal and collective unconscious), keeping the beta and alpha states active via confusion is essential while we deepen to theta, our working state. For example, we could use a

play on words about 'the present': *". . . as you think about the present, and the present you're giving yourself, by presenting here today, while the future that is tomorrow, means tomorrow presents itself after today, and when you're fully immersed in this day as you are now, then you make the present in today be the past. And maybe you feel a little bit lost and drifting afar, as you wonder where in time you presently are? . . ."*

4. **Deepening process** – We then utilise between three to six hypnotic deepening procedures. Once in hypnosis, deepeners are a way of guiding someone into an even deeper hypnotic state, thus affecting the brain states and moving to the frequency required for the work – theta state. A common example is guiding someone down a flight of stairs. With each step down, the suggestion of becoming more deeply relaxed is given, compounding the previous suggestion of deeper relaxation for as many steps as is needed. You can also use the image of moving down floors in a lift or escalator. Depending on the responses of the individual this should ideally take around twenty minutes, which is traditionally longer than most hypnotherapeutic inductions. Such is the need in past life therapy work that you suspend the logical rational mind for the amount of time needed for the past life exploration.

Throughout this process, there is a constant reference to the words 'back', 'small(er)', 'younger', and 'time'. The mention of 'back' is utilised so that when you start going 'back in time' there has already been many pre-suggestions referring to 'back', so there are as few jolts for the rational mind during the regression process as possible. This seeds the mind to regress back through time. For example, during the body relaxation you concentrate on the experience of the back of each leg, and the back of each arm, and relaxing the back area, and you may even suggest that they move the waves of relaxation back down the arm and back up again.

The suggestion of 'smaller' should be used in preparation for the regression back in time with the suggestions of getting 'younger' in age, eventually to the womb. For example, in one of the deepeners you may suggest the taking of 'small steps' or you ask them to notice the 'small changes' within them as they relax even deeper, including noticing that as they become 'smaller' and (therefore) 'younger', they're aware of how 'small and young' they are becoming.

Notice how much the hypnotic part of the process engages in a play on words. When you learn how to master the complexity of language, you realise how much power words have and by how much they shape what your mind perceives and believes. To delve into the power of hypnotic language even further, see Erickson (1991).

'Time' is also a word to frequently use to prepare the mind for going back in time, so you suggest, for example, that they 'take their time', and 'take time to allow themselves to relax completely', noticing those occasions when 'time feels like it stands still'. This play on words is a linguistic moving melody which creates confusion, this in turn compounding the trance depth and opening the mind further into the journey of desired discovery. Sometimes just reading these words can impact the reader, shifting them in time, taking them back to their younger, smaller self, when times were different.

When talking about time, it is important to consider the 'time distortion' process. The very nature of past life therapy involves distorting the regular perspective of linear time, which we discussed in Chapter 4. Therefore, it's important to suggest that time will become distorted early on in the hypnotic trance process. Time distortion is an incredible hypnotic deepener. It disengages you from logic like no other deepener we know.

Imagine you entered into this past-life journey with a logical, rational mind . . . It just wouldn't work. It wouldn't make any sense. We need to use an induction that takes you as far away from logic as possible, and time distortion does a profound job of doing just that. In practice we ask clients to imagine or actually hear (we recommend that you have a clock present) the sound of a ticking clock and suggest that they notice how the ticking of the clock seems to slow down, slowing down time as well. We can use the sound to play with time, then suggesting the speeding up of the ticking of the clock again, moving time forward a day, and back then a week, and then a month, or three, or seven weeks and one day to a Tuesday, or Friday, or was it Wednesday? . . . all the time moulding the perception of awareness to where our work is heading . . . the *past*.

Throughout the process, it's really important for you to travel on this journey in your own mind as well. You are going with the client on their voyage to their other world. Imagine it all yourself as you say it – 'as if' you were their companion on the journey. You see, *your* logic is not useful here either. Of course, you need to guide them in the process, but you also need to suspend a large part of your understanding and just join their ride and be there with them as they explore this other world.

Remember when we said at the beginning of this book that we'd met before? That implies that you and the client are on this incredible journey to past ancient times – you also have met before. That's why you're together doing this. It was meant to be. You've something to learn from each other. You might not know what that is yet, but if you allow yourself to go along with this, you might just learn a life lesson that changes everything.

5. **Next you begin to move the experience back in this life**, regressing them to being younger and younger, smaller and smaller, suggesting that as they get younger and younger they notice their body getting smaller and smaller. This is known as the regression (or affect) bridge. There are a lot of different ways you can use a regression bridge. You can guide someone to imagine looking at a calendar and see the pages of the calendar where the days are flying off into the wind, revealing the

previous days one by one; you can use a train metaphor with the train going backwards in time; or you can simply suggest going back five years at a time, as if every five years was a season in somebody's life . . . summer, autumn, winter, and spring, each season five years earlier.

This first part of the regression involves taking the client back through this life as far back as that familiar, dark, warm, safe place – the womb. It's the beginning of time; it always has been and will always be. From there we have to make a transition to the past life.

One of the ways we've found most effective is using the analogy of the white light, a pinprick of white, glowing light. So, from the womb, seeing the white light, moving towards it, being drawn close and reaching out into it. It's an enticing image as we suggest that this light leads them to the past life they are about to explore. The light is the conduit to lives both past and future.

Transitions in behaviour and experience are most successfully gained through small incremental stages – a step at a time – or by successive approximations – gradually narrowing the focus. In our work we use numbers, helping our client to stage the transition in their journey step-by-step as we guide them into their past life. In practice this might sound like, "What I am going to do now is count to three, and when I count to three you will find the light . . . one, two, three [*snaps fingers*] . . . and you *have* the light there . . . where is it, to your left or your right?" The piece-by-piece creation of their inner journey designs the movement through the internal shift that they need to go through. It manages in a sequential manner a state change, which is what we're wanting to create.

Each one of these steps are important when preparing to regress back into a past life experience.

Regression

To explore our past lives, we need to regress back into them. Regression is a common experience for many people. For example, you could act like a teenager again, with that 'I don't care what you think' attitude towards your boss, storming out of their office, slamming the door as you go! Or you might regress to being six years of age, having a tantrum with your friend or partner because you can't have your own way. You may also re-experience the freedom of your youth when you are out in nature on a long summer's day walk.

In therapy, we are able to purposely regress someone into their past to uncover the roots of a presenting problem. The aim in doing this is to release the emotional charge that is stuck within a past repressed event and which subsequently interrupts the flow of life. By working through the event and gaining a more accurate account of what actually happened, we experience an emotional release.

This kind of regression work helps us with an inner 'growing-up' process. It facilitates the maturation of a part of us that was suspended or split away at the time of the event. The intense thoughts and feelings led to the need for psychological repression of that experience. This is where we push the event down into our unconscious mind so as to protect us from dealing with the enormity of it. In revisiting our own experiences of this, Sandra remembers her time as a qualified physical education teacher, driving a minibus with her Year 7 and 8 Netball teams to a fixture and feeling far too young to be taking on such a responsibility. There was still an immature part of her stuck in a past trauma and not yet grown up. Experiencing therapeutic regression helped mature that part of her up closer to her chronological age at the time.

Do you feel sometimes you have never fully grown up? Are there times when a part of you feels quite childlike, or certainly younger than you are?

Take a look at your different ages:

- Your biological age

Now think about how old you feel for the following:

- Psychological age

- Physical age
- Emotional age
- Spiritual age

Are they all the same or different? How much do you think your past has impacted these? Make some notes of key events and how they might have stuck some part of you back at that time.

When we think about our childhood and its effects on us, we inevitably hold inaccurate or biased accounts of events, as our meaning-making, understanding, and logic is relative to the age we were. It's from these skewed recollections that we create various learnings, often self-critical or deprecating in their nature – necessary, however, for our survival – and it's these which affect what we believe and how we think and behave as adults. For example, we might form the belief as a child that we were responsible for the separation of our parents in some way, which may then be carried into adulthood as a belief of "I am too much", or "I am not enough". This can lead us to denying ourselves friendships or intimate partners as we project these beliefs onto these adult relationships.

Regression can help re-address currently held beliefs that limit your life, and allow you the safe opportunity to be angry, upset, scared, or whatever other feelings need to be felt again. Once you have gone back to a particular significant time and experienced it as if it were happening right now through the process of revivification – where you re-experience what happened then just *as it was*, and more accurately – you can realise and then release the locked-up emotion and be re-informed about that situation. You then bring this information back to your present-day self. This is a really powerful and effective way of healing and maturing this part of you.

There are different types of regression that we can use in therapy. Some of them can be planned, such as when you are working therapeutically on an issue using a specific regression method like the 'affect bridge' or 'the 'library' technique (see Barber and Westland, 2010), whilst others can happen spontaneously, for example, when the client experiences childlike emotional responses and acts much younger than their years. This can then be explored and worked with during the session. It is also possible to have an intentionally planned past life regression therapy session, or you find that during a hypnotherapy session the client has spontaneously regressed into a past life. As you read in Chapter 3, this has happened to both of us in our sessions with clients.

The point of exploring the process of regression and past lives is not just so we can experience once upon a time being Henry VIII or Anne Boleyn. Although that might sound fantastically exciting, the more practical purpose is to find some answers to presenting life issues, to release emotional blockages, and to come to some resolution within ourselves.

PLTT is a way to reveal and heal karmic grooves and revise aspects of yourself. It's about discovery, transformation, aligning to your purpose and gaining fresh clarity and direction in your life.

CONTRAINDICATIONS

At this point we need to talk about safety. There will be occasions when using past life therapy is not in the best interests of the client. Therefore, we need to examine some contraindications for this work.

We do have a few issues with the nature of contraindications, as we feel it pigeonholes people too much in terms of classifying psychological states. Nevertheless, it gives you important awareness in thinking about taking care of whoever you take through this process of past life therapy. Using this technique *could* be psychologically dangerous. Therefore, it would be irresponsible not to know when you should not be engaging in this work. So, to that end, let's look at what conditions are not suitable for this method of discovery.

In general, you will be working with people with a sound mind – those who can't get lost (psychologically) in another life and find it difficult or impossible to return to their present day here and now. Therefore, one contraindication for past life therapy is working with people who are unable to think rationally and logically on a consistent basis. Conditions such as Schizophrenia, Personality Disorders, Dissociative and Bipolar Disorders, and PTSD, might, for somebody who has these kinds of diagnoses, exacerbate their inability to exist here in their present reality. Generally, those who are suffering from delusions, hallucinations, and flashbacks should not engage in past life therapy. It's important that we keep people who are experiencing these kinds of states of mind safely rooted in the reality of now.

People who are taking psychoactive medication, such as beta-blockers, which stop or reduce the body's natural fight-or-flight responses, and those suffering with heart problems, epilepsy, or who are pregnant are also contraindicated, as there is no way of knowing how these people will react to the intense emotions and profound realisations that can be experienced in past life therapy work.

You should also be mindful of using this approach with people who are diagnosed with anorexia, and clinical depression. Again, in this work we are stepping out of a universally accepted reality, and for people experiencing these issues, it could be dangerous to do so. This applies also to regular recreational drug users who might have experienced alternative reality states or those who regularly consume very large amounts of alcohol. The reason for this is that in past life therapy we are working with altered states of consciousness, and so a strong ability to retain a connection to current reality is important for safe practice.

When you enter into a past life experience, you will during the process be going through the past life death transition, and this can sometimes be traumatic. This is often one of the most illuminating pointers to your present life behaviours, challenges, and issues – so it's not a bad thing; it is an enormous learning opportunity and for most it is a release from that life. As British psychologist and past life therapy author Andy Tomlinson (2006) writes of the Buddhist belief, "Dying is seen as a great opportunity for people to come to terms with their whole lives, and to their own deepest truth" (p. 65). But, bear in mind that as this happens, physically someone can become panicky and show signs of distress.

In summary, the reason that it's important to be aware of these points is that we don't want to exacerbate any underling conditions. Past life therapy is about healing, clarity, understanding, and increased awareness and insight. As long as you work safely, then what you can discover can be both revelatory and life changing.

Let's begin this process by experiencing a past life journey, where you can connect with your own past life presence and discover who you were, where you lived in the world, and when else you have existed in time.

WHERE IN THE WORLD?

To get you connected to your previous lives, take a look at the map of the world on the next page (Figure 6.1). In Chapter 5, you engaged in some conscious exploration of the world, but now we want you to go a little deeper by accessing your unconscious awareness.

As you look at the map . . . just staring at it for a moment, begin moving your eyes over the whole image, noting all the different continents and countries and also noticing how you're feeling and what is happening in your body. Remember the places you have already visited in your life and remind yourself of what they were like.

Figure 6.1

Every place has a different feel, a different energy about it, so remember what that was like for you when you went to a particular country. Then choose another country that you haven't been to before and consider what you imagine it might be like. We have heard many people say that going to India is a complete culture shock, with such a different energy – one they'd never imagined until they went there. But even if you've never travelled to India, you can still imagine what it might be like for you. It has been described to us as "an overload on all of one's senses in one moment". Imagine setting foot on Indian soil for a few moments. Feel what it might be like to connect with the sounds, smells, and colours . . . and imagine soaking it up. Does it impact your energy and vibrations, or is there another country that you imagine doing that for you?

Imagine traveling in your mind to other countries in the same way and see what happens for you. Where are you drawn towards, and what do you imagine it would be like for you? How would your senses be affected there? Record your thoughts in your workbook.

Now take another look at the map. Where in the world do you feel repelled from, and what images come to mind in that place? This might not make logical sense yet. This may be because there is some unpleasant past life unfinished business there, so just ponder for a while and explore the places you are not wanting to go to, and then write a few words about your thoughts.

Now let's further your exploration, at a deeper level.

Experiencing the Journey

Now that you have reached this place, we're going to take you through a hypnotic induction to relax your body and settle you into your creative mind. Then we're going to take you on a journey that will lead you to embodying a character from one of your past lives. As we take this journey together, we will guide you to travel across the world and back in time to find a past incarnation of 'you', to see what you were like there. After that we will guide you back in your mind to the here and now to process your learning. We have used this visualisation many times before in one-to-one sessions and group workshops, and people find this incredibly thought provoking and meaningful. As you allow yourself to connect with the visualisation, if you feel you are forcing yourself to find something and be someone, remember, it's all coming from somewhere within you.

Check in with how you feel right now. Then make yourself comfortable, and let the journey begin.

As with the previous visualisation, please make sure that you are not going to be disturbed for a while – the experience takes around twenty minutes. First turn off any devices that could interrupt. You need to ensure that you are not doing anything else other than reading the guided visualisation or listening to it if you prefer (at www.healingfromtheotherside.com). It is best to listen to the visualisation so you can truly immerse yourself into the experience and let it unfold naturally. Once you have started we advise that you keep going until the end. Settle back and allow yourself to become curious. We are not going to use the full hypnotic induction for past life therapy in this instance because we first want you to get accustomed to the process in order to get a sense of what past life therapy is like.

The Journey through Time around the World – The Visualisation

As we explained in Chapter 2, if you are reading the following script you'll notice that we occasionally pause [. . .] for a short while

. . . and then continue, just as in this sentence. This is to give you time to drift with the visualisation and see what comes up for you. Let's begin.

Okay, so, when you are ready, just close your eyes and take a nice deep breath in and simply concentrate on the following words . . . and that's all we want you to do . . . is to concentrate on your breathing . . . and as you breathe in, imagine that you breathe in a deep sense of calmness and peace . . . and with each breath that you breathe out, that deep sense of calmness and peace . . . just simply begins to flow through your body. As it flows through your body, just imagine that inner eye inside your mind gently beginning to close down, shutting out all stray thoughts and images that you simply don't want to interfere with how relaxed, calm, and peaceful you can become.

We want you just to allow that feeling to continue to flow through you. From the top of your head down to the tips of your toes . . . and then flowing from the tips of your toes and moving gently up through each different part of your body . . . and as you follow it, moving through your toes and your feet . . . and your ankles and your calves, and your shins . . . as you follow it, you continue to focus on these words. Of course, you can be aware of the different sounds around you occasionally from inside the room . . . and maybe from outside . . . as you become aware of those different sounds, just knowing that the only sound that you really need to be aware of is the sound of your voice inside your mind as you read these words . . . as that wave of calmness and peace just simply flows all the way through you . . . through your calves and your shins and your knees and through your thigh muscles. And all around your waist and your hips, experiencing a wonderful sense of peace and stillness . . . continuing to move through you.

And in your mind, counting back through those numbers. Starting at any number you wish. Choosing a number and beginning to count backwards quietly inside your mind . . . and with each count down, noticing . . . noticing that as the numbers get lower, your relaxation becomes deeper.

And as your relaxation becomes deeper, the numbers simply get lower . . . and lower . . . And that wave of calmness and peace just gently flows.

And then . . . then it moves right the way up through your lower back . . . and as it moves through your lower back . . . imagine it moving up through the muscles on each side of your spine and your body. Drifting through your whole back, through the muscles on each side of your spine, up through your middle back . . . into your upper back . . . and as it goes through your back, going back, it moves then through into your shoulders . . . and that feeling continues right the way through your back and your shoulders . . . and then down through your body . . . centring in your stomach muscles . . . and the whole of your body feels that wave of calmness and peace, just continuing to flow through you.

And in a moment, you start to imagine the ticking of a clock. Notice each second ticking . . . passing by . . . and as that small hand on the clock ticks and ticks away . . . I want you to imagine that each second begins to spread out and become longer. Each second becomes ten seconds. And each ten seconds becomes thirty seconds. Time begins to slow down . . . like it did . . . in summertime, when you were much younger . . . when the holidays seemed to last forever . . . and as that time begins to spread out, imagine that you flip the clock around . . . and that tick . . . tick . . . tick . . . begins to move backwards through time. And as it moves backwards through time . . . it goes back further and further through time . . . time just drifts and wonders . . . and at the same time, that feeling of calmness and peace continues to flow through you . . . through your fingers and thumbs and hands and wrists and forearms . . . and into your elbows and your upper arms and shoulders . . . time just slowing everything down deeper . . . and deeper.

And that feeling begins to move further . . . up through your arms and your shoulders . . . through your neck . . . and around the back of your head. And through your scalp and your forehead and your eyes and your eyelids. And your face and your jaw . . . relax even more.

And then your mind and your body begin to drift, and imagine drifting up, out of the place you're in . . . higher out of that place and up into the sky . . . safely drifting up into the sky. And drifting higher so you see beneath you . . . getting farther away . . . moving somewhere else through time . . . and you wonder whether the ticking of the clock goes forwards or backwards, backwards or forwards . . . and it doesn't really matter . . . because it's just mind over matter. Or is it matter over mind, as the time ticks by? And you drift higher and deeper . . . you become calmer . . . as we begin our journey around the world.

And in your imagination now . . . imagining that you're like a satellite . . . traveling and spinning above and around the world . . . looking down . . . and checking out each of the countries, one . . . by one . . . and making a note of the ones that you're positively drawn to . . . and there doesn't need to be any logical reason why you're attracted to them . . . you just travel around the world . . . and examine each country . . . taking your time . . . slowing down . . . and as you take your time, and it slows down . . . you note the countries that you're drawn to . . . just check them out one by one. Something about some countries that attracts you . . . that pulls you . . . and on that journey . . . I want you to also make a note of all the countries that you would prefer to avoid. Checking out each country one by one. Something about some countries that you prefer . . . and some countries that you prefer to avoid . . . noting where they are . . . and their name . . . and moving on.

Keep moving through the journey. And as you do . . . one of those countries . . . has the strongest charge. You go around the world, checking each country one by one, and something about one country has the most powerful pull. And I want you just to be there . . . aware of hovering above that country . . . and then, very slowly . . . coming down slowly . . . drawn to a particular part of that country. Continuing to slowly descend . . . getting closer to that scene . . . in your past life. Slowly settling into your body . . . in that past life. Landing into that body.

And when you're there . . . you look down . . . and you become aware of what you have on your feet. You become aware of the clothes that you're wearing . . . or maybe you are not wearing. What's on your body? What's happening around you? Note if you are by yourself or with other people . . . and you notice what's happening there . . . just letting that become stronger . . . and clearer . . . and clearer and stronger . . . as you settle fully. As you settle fully into your body.

And in that life . . . in your own time . . . you notice who you are there. You notice what you do next. And you might have a sense of who you are, the name you've been given. You might have a sense of your age . . . and you might know it or just . . . have a sense of it. Get a feel for the era you're in. Just notice what you notice there. Noticing whether you're male or female . . . and who else is around you. You might get a year . . . an era . . . a time . . . or just know where and when that is . . . and it's there to revisit. That 'you' is there, it's here, for a reason. And you begin to get a sense of what that is . . . that reason . . . and you just ponder on that for a few moments.

We're going to revisit that place, or maybe another place. But for now . . . for now though . . . begin to feel yourself floating up . . . out of that body . . . there's work to be done there, a journey to unfold. But for now . . . you rise up out of that body. And you float back up . . . you float back up . . . and feel it around you . . . feel the energy . . . the connection . . . and then you notice that it's not even something else . . . that energy is you, and you are it . . . and find yourself then . . . like that satellite, floating around the earth. And then you begin to move back towards this place . . . in this time . . . beginning to hear the ticking of the clock again in your mind . . . each tick, a second passing through time . . . getting closer and closer to now . . . as you float down back into you . . . back into your body here, now, in this time and this space.

And then when you're ready . . . very gently just letting your eyes . . . gently open . . . as you become fully alert, fully aware . . . and here . . . fully present . . . and fully aware.

Welcome back! We hope you enjoyed the ride. Take some time now to record below your experience: What happened? Where did you go? Who were you? How did you feel? What meaning in your present life might this have illuminated?

We hope this has given you some things to think about. We would love to hear about your experience. If you would like to get some feedback, please feel free to share your experience and what you discovered on your journey around the world in our Facebook group, a link to which is at www.healingfromtheotherside.com. You can also read there about other readers' journeys and reach out to some likeminded people. Whatever you experienced is meaningful for you in some way, and you may benefit from exploring this with somebody else on another unique journey. You never know who you'll connect with and who *they* might have been in your previous lives.

So, you have now experienced a simplified version of the hypnotic induction, and have experienced going back and embodying a past life character and establishing a past life scene. Let's keep moving further into the process in the next chapter, to where the real healing begins, as we step into the past life experience and examine what life held for us there.

CHAPTER 8
PAST LIFE TRANSPERSONAL THERAPY
THE PAST LIFE

The mysteries of universe are revealed to those who seek to know the truth of their own existence first.
Anjali Chugh

THE PAST LIFE TRANSPERSONAL THERAPY PROCESS

In the previous chapter you experienced a visualisation that introduced you to the first three steps of the PLTT process, as shown below. This included the hypnotic induction, embodying a past life character, and establishing the scene you were in, garnering details that helped you connect to that time and place. Let's explore further now steps 4 and 5, where we find out the story of the past life and how someone died.

The steps covered so far are:

1. The hypnotic induction and regression techniques specific to Past Life Transpersonal Therapy.

2. Embodiment of the past life character. Keeping in the 'past-present' tense and in the past life body.
3. Establishing the scene in detail: Where are you? Who else is there? What do you see? When is this? What year? What else?

We will first explore how to work in stages 1 - 3 and then move to the following steps.

4. Exploring the past life. How the life is lived and develops, examining any poignant moments.
5. Moving to the moment of death and discovery of what's taken from this life through to the death transition.

Embodying the Character and Describing the Scene

Once you have taken someone into their past life character, you need to help them fully embody him or her and have them describe where they are. Make sure they are looking out of their own eyes and moving their own limbs. We really want them to associate into the character rather than watching themselves as if in a movie or as a bystander observing the scene (which would indicate a dissociated perspective). Don't assume that there will be an automatic association into the character. Remember that your work is to guide them into accessing their embodied experience as if they were associated into it and experiencing it in that way. Remember that people are extremely suggestable at this stage, so your expectant tone is important. Speak in a way that emphasises the naturalness of what you are asking them to do and in a soft, supportive way.

It is really important to use the *present tense* and also keep them describing in the 'I' rather than 'he' or 'she' – as this will keep them in the experience as it is happening to them in the moment. To do this you need to ask questions such as, "What are *you* wearing as you are looking down?" "How are *you* feeling right now?" or "What's happening there for *you*?"

Establish the character and where they are, using both closed and open questions. Closed questions enable focus onto the detail of the experience, such as their clothing, surroundings, and other people. Open questions encourage a deeper and freer connection at the feeling, belief, and value level.

Always repeat back what has been said, as it keeps them associated and embodied in the experience as they hear their own words. This also gives them the opportunity to add to the detail if they need to. Leave a pause between you repeating what they have said and asking the next question.

Examples of Closed Questions

- As you look down at your feet, what are you wearing?
- Looking up at your legs, what do you have on?
- Beginning to describe your upper body – what are you wearing?
- Are you alone or with others?
- How old do you *feel* there? (Not how old *are* you? This can alert logic.)
- What is the year? (If they are young they may not know this.)

Examples of Open Questions

- What is that like?
- Where are you there?
- How is that?
- Notice looking around you, and what are you seeing?
- How are you feeling about what you are doing?
- What's really important for you right now?
- What's troubling you?
- How do you feel about your life?

As you explore the present scene, elicit what they are thinking and feeling about where they are in their life and what they are doing in it. Stay exactly with them in their experience. Remember that everything is relevant even if you feel that it is trivial or you don't quite understand it. We don't know yet what is ahead of them after this moment in their past life, so keep probing to get the finer detail and above all, be curious.

In your questioning, your task is to elicit as much information as possible. There can, however, be a danger in leading someone with questions that reflect your own preconceived ideas that arise from the unfolding story. That is why it is important to use the kind of open questions above to guide the person through their experience (Scheflin and Shapiro, 1989; Hunter and Eimer, 2012) rather than focusing them onto something specific.

Once you have an understanding of where they are in their past life and what they are doing, you need to move them on. Initially we move them forwards through small segments of time within the scene that they are exploring. Imagine that they are telling you that they are dressed in cloth, with no shoes on, and they are a young boy of nine years of age, and on their own. They don't know their own family as they were sold to the family they are now serving, and they have been a servant for as long as they can remember. They are totally alone, and they are carrying their master's clothes as they walk along a dusty path. It is a pilgrimage.

From here you would suggest to them, "In a moment I am going to count to three and snap my fingers, and you will have transported a few hours forward in time there . . . one, two, three [*snap*] . . . and what's happening there?"

Staying in the scenario, they then go on to describe that they have been walking for hours and hours, and they are very tired and hungry. This scenario was an actual experience that one of Sandra's clients described, having presented to her for therapy, suffering with the symptoms of ME.

Once you have explored this time in more depth, move them forwards in age. Suggest to them that on the count of three they'll move forwards again, this time a couple of years from where they are, and then . . . one, two, three [*snap*], and ask, "Where are you in your life there?" and gather some specific details about what's happening. Do exactly the same exploration as before, enquiring about "What is it like?" "How are you feeling?" "What's really important for you here?" "What is concerning for you?" "What would you like to do in your future?" and "What do you dream of?" The boy is now 13 and works harder and harder each day fetching and carrying for his master. Survival is all that concerns him while he secretly dreams of escaping one day and finding out who his real family are and why he ended up enslaved.

Allow yourself to be curious and ask questions that link to the previous part of their life that you have just explored. For example, if you discovered someone having a child and when you move on in time they don't mention their child, you might ask, "And where is your child there?" We gather the information to build up a great sense of this past life: the relationships, the lifestyle, the emotions experienced, the hopes and dreams, the regrets in all that was lived – as this will help in revealing the unfinished business.

Use direct suggestions to move backwards and forwards through the past life to gather information. These suggestions can include, "and as I count to three, you'll move further through (or back) in time. One, two, three [*snap*]." Follow your intuition if you feel there is something that has been missed.

The Last Day of Your Life

Once you have explored the past life, you then guide them towards their death. You ask them to move to the last day of their life and then to a time just before they take their last breath . . . and then explore what's happening there. What thoughts do they die with? What feelings do they leave that life with? What meaning do they take from the nature of their death? The boy is now a young man of 23 who has made his escape. He is running and running to get away as two men chase him. He manages to out run them, but he collapses with total exhaustion, and it is here as he lays on a hot dusty road that he takes his last breath. He dies feeling aggrieved that he never had the freedom to be himself and that he never knew why his family sent him to this miserable and hard life.

You then guide them through to their passing, where they leave their past life body form. Ask them to hover over the body in their soul state. Here they gain awareness of their immortal soul, which can make a painful passing easier. From there they transcend to the spirit realm.

It is crucial that you allow them to move through this phase, because it is here that the unfinished business is revealed and knowledge of what is taken with them. Woolger (1988) writes, ". . . consciousness is at the highest degree of intensity at death, with the result that thoughts and feelings that occur in this transition are deeply imprinted on the transmigrating consciousness" (p. 273). Therefore, we need gain clarity around these moments as we move through the death transition and into the spirit realm.

Your Transformation

At this stage in the process, you have arrived at the end of one particular past life and are now within the spirit realm, where the healing and learning takes place. Here you begin to enter the realm of transformation, readying the move from one life to the next.

What is transformation or change for you? At certain junctions in life, change of some kind becomes pressing or impossible to deny. Some people desire to change an aspect of their self, such as becoming more confident or less anxious. Some look longingly at their transformation, waiting for something to come from the outside material world, like a lucky break, believing their personal growth lies in acquiring more belongings or wealth. Others find themselves in a life-altering experience, where transformation comes in the form of a rebirth of their sense of self and their purpose and meaning. This can lead to the turning to religion, changing career, or taking up the fight for a just cause. Transformation comes in many different forms, and this is also inherent in the idea of moving from one life to another life.

Jung and Transformation

In *Four Archetypes* (2004, p. 53–56), Jung contemplates five different definitions, all of which offer insight into what happens in the spirit realm as we prepare for the next incarnation. A core theme of all five forms is that, through the process of death and rebirth, we may come to realise that which is essential within us.

1. **Metempsychosis, or Transmigration of Souls:** Our life is prolonged in time by passing through different bodily existences, a continuous life sequence interrupted by different reincarnations. What this means is that life is one continuum where our soul is being transmuted from life to life carrying karma through different bodily existences.

2. **Reincarnation:** This concept of rebirth suggests there is a continuity of personality. The same personality exists on a continuum and is accessible to memory, so that when you are born, you are potentially able to remember that you have lived through previous life experiences and that these were your past lives.

3. **Resurrection:** This refers to the re-establishment of existence after one's death in the human form. The resurrected being may be a different one, so you're not reborn into another version of you, living a different existence to fulfil some sense of karma, but you are resurrected into something else.

4. **Rebirth:** This is rebirth within the span of an individual's life and is more of a renewal without any change of being. The personality which is renewed is not wholly changed – only parts of the personality, which are subjected to strengthening, improvement or healing (emotional and physical).

Rebirthing is a powerful process, one, that if you experience it, will undoubtedly have a profound impact on you. Tom has been lucky enough to have worked with the renowned American doctor, author, and clown (yes, clown) Patch Adams in Russia, where he engaged with some rebirthing work. Patch is a medical doctor and founder of the US-based Gesundheit Institute, which aims to "reframe and reclaim the concept of 'hospital'". The Institute is a holistic medical care centre focusing on helping people heal and providing them with hope in some of their darkest moments. If you've seen the movie *Patch Adams* (dir: Tom Shadyac, 1998), you'll know he did some crazy things – like bathing people in noodles – really crazy stuff that actually gave people who were sick hope and lifted their spirits. The work Patch continues to do is incredible because it helps people by utilising the power of belief and hope. If you get a chance to watch *Patch Adams*, then do so – it's an inspirational story. To find out more about the work Patch is doing around the world, see www.patchadams.org.

The rebirthing work Tom did aims to release the birth trauma by actually reenacting the experience of being reborn in *this* life, in terms of you and your behaviours and your character . . . all of who you are. You experience a powerful catharsis. Tom got the feeling of being refreshed, revived, and that something was 'new'. It's a fascinating encounter as something becomes pure again from within you. To find out more, see Taylor (1994) and Grof & Grof (2010).

5. **Participation in the process of transformation:** Jung's fifth form is indirect rebirth, where transformation is brought by passing through death and rebirth in a more indirect manner, such as through participating in a process or rite of transformation, such as the Christian Mass or some pagan practices.

These ideas of rebirthing and transformation can give a real *essence* of what is carried from one life to another. As Jung writes (2004, p. 57), "We are not concerned here with the question: is rebirth a tangible process of some sort?" but more about discovering how you relate to the process of transformation in your past lives. Can we prove it? Do we need to? As Jung succinctly continues, "The mere fact that people talk about rebirth, and that there is such a concept at all, means that a store of psychic experiences designated by that term must actually exist" (p. 50). If something feels real for you, it resides within your reality.

Commitment to the Process

As experienced therapists and trainers ourselves, we place great importance on working safely from a psychological perspective. There can be dangers when using this method if you don't cover all the various aspects of the process to at least beyond the death transition. For example, it would not be safe if you leave someone at the stage of their death with an unexpressed emotion, or you pull them out of the death transition too soon without clarifying meaning. There is a need to integrate them back into this life and the present, or you risk leaving a part of them stuck in the past. Therefore, it's important to make sure that no matter how emotional things get, you continue through from steps 1 to 5. This asks you to appreciate your own emotional self and how you are when powerful emotions are experienced by others and expressed. If you have difficulties when people get upset, distressed or angry, then it may be wise to make this the very first thing you decide to work on in your own journey of healing.

If you take someone to their death and end the session before moving beyond this, then you simply leave that person experiencing their emotional past life with an unresolved trauma, having brought it back into their present. However, if you have explored their past life, and taken your time moving through to the death experience, the meanings discovered and any unfinished business that has become their karma, will become clear and resolvable.

You can appreciate then that you need to be ready for the power of this work. When someone is going through the death transition, it can be an intense experience for them – and it may be for you also. So you need to be prepared. Not all people experiencing past life therapy go through an extreme catharsis, where they release powerful repressed emotions, but nevertheless, you will feel what they're experiencing to a greater or lesser degree. This is an important point for you to consider because you need to be able to deal with *your* feelings as well as *theirs* at the same time, in order to safely guide them through the experience.

It is the most rewarding work releasing someone from what is holding them back, so hold on to knowing the relief that comes from unlocking and unblocking that which has been stored away, sometimes for a very long time. When you do this work, you need to go through it, rather than just get so far and think, "Oh no, this is getting too emotional, we had better stop."

In the next chapter, we will look at how the PLTT process works in finer detail, as we explore a session that takes a client into their past life and opens them up to exploring what happened there, right through to the death transition. If you would prefer to watch the video recording of this session, then you can access this at www.healingfromtheotherside.com.

Chapter 9
In Action
Exploring the Past Life World

The secret to happiness is freedom
. . . and the secret to freedom is courage.
Thucydides

Prea

In this chapter we will explore the past life experience and the powerful connection it realises for a client in an actual session. At the beginning of this book, we introduced you to Prea. We now return to her story and show you exactly how her past life journey unfolded.

Introduction

If you recall from the beginning of the book, Prea was looking to make changes in her life and relationships but felt blocked. After trying counselling, she was still struggling to take the steps she needed to make these changes happen. Something was blocking her and she couldn't get to the bottom of it. She felt that there was some kind of unfinished business between her and her partner.

In Prea's session, in which she chose to participate as a training demonstration during one of our Past Life Transpersonal Therapy courses, our aim was to show the first phase of the PLTT process. This is where we begin to explore the past life, as we work to establish and then embody the past life character, as well as getting a description of the past life scene. As you will see in Prea's session below, we then moved to the moment of death so that she could elucidate the unfinished business. Finally, when she was brought out of the experience and the hypnotic trance, we took some time to explore and process what she had discovered and what this meant to her.

PREA'S PAST LIFE SESSION

What follows is the full account of Prea's session.

Therapist: To start the session, what would you like to get out of it? There's a reason that you've been drawn to it?

Prea: Yes. There is.

Therapist: Okay. Would you mind telling me more?

Prea: It's about looking at repeat patterns that I go through and that I can't quite get to the bottom of. Why even though I've had counselling and done some other investigations, there seems to be still something. It's like I call it a 'karma tie', particularly in relationships that I feel that I can't quite break. So that's what I would like to look at.

Therapist: Okay. That sounds like in relationships there's something you want to be able to break away from?

Prea: Yes. Absolutely.

Therapist: So, in terms of this historically throughout your life, is this something that's always been around for a long time?

Prea: I've probably had the experience twice. But the last experience is the hardest one to break really. It's still a little bit ongoing.

Therapist: So it's still quite present and I get the sense it's still quite raw.

Prea: Yeah, a little. Yeah.

Therapist: Alright. So, it's difficult to let go?

Prea: Yeah.

Therapist: And you mentioned it in terms of a 'karma tie'. So, you feel like there's something that's hard to unlink. Are you able to say more about that?

Prea: Yeah. It's a relationship I had with somebody, and it's kind of been on-off, on-off, and it keeps coming in and out of my life. There was a very, very strong connection between us, and we had what I thought were some unusual experiences where we had sort of simultaneous dreams. We seemed to have a sense of each other from a previous connection and we both felt it very much. Neither of us have had this before with anybody else. I'd also been to a psychic about it and she seemed to think that we had had a connection in the past, that we had some unfinished business. But I don't know what the unfinished business is and it'd be really great to find out to finish it.

Therapist: But there's something there that you feel. I suppose, in a way, what I'm picking up is that it's hard to unlink from somebody when there's something not quite fulfilled or not quite finished.

Prea: And it doesn't feel like it's to do with the 'now' because in terms of a 'now' relationship, yes, we've acknowledged that there are things that aren't quite right, and we're not compatible in many ways, and we have different views. But yet, there's a glue that sticks us, that we can't seem to wriggle away from. Does it make sense?

Therapist: Yes, it does. It makes total sense. I think you've explained it incredibly clearly. So, in relation to that, if you think about that in your life and your past lives, are you making any links?

Prea: I did have a dream, like I said, and it was a dream that this guy had as well. And it was before we got together when we were just friends.

It was very strange because I was in Japan, probably, medieval Japan, and I was in this burning building, and everything was muddy. There was a lot of a sense of smell, lots of rush, and this particular man came up to me on a horse, and it was a kind of a 'good-bye' scenario. But I was very overcome by the fact of the violence of the situation. It was a lot of chaos and violence. I've never had a dream like this before.

I remember having very, very long hair, and I was kind of like pushed away, and he rode off. That was the last I saw. I think something bad happened to me after that. But I don't know because I woke up. But I feel that that was a pivotal moment.

Then when we'd done the other work with the shadow [*Jung*], when we've looked at the shadow side, I always come across this Japanese woman with the long hair, and I'm quite angry. I think the two are interconnected somehow. It's strange.

Therapist: Okay. It certainly sounds very vivid.

Prea: It could be my imagination, but I don't think so because it was the senses . . . like . . . normally, when you dream, you don't smell things or taste things, and it was very strong in that one. It was multi-sensory.

Therapist: Yeah. It sounds like it was very visceral experience on, as you say, lots of levels, which is more than just visualising or picturing something and imagining it like that.

Prea: He didn't look the same [*the man on the horse*]. I knew it was him. I recognize the energy of him but he was very different in appearance.

Therapist: We've got some really good background here, and what sounds important is that you recognise you – it sounds like you know that you're carrying something not from this life but from somewhere else because you haven't had that experience in this life, right?

Prea: No.

Therapist: Let's explore it, shall we? We'll see where we end up, and we'll see where we'll go. Then, we'll work through it and see how we can take what you feel you're carrying and how it's relative to this 'karma tie' that you've described, and how potentially that is keeping you in this place. Because it sounds like what you'd like to do actually is to break that, and break it in a way to bring that pattern or that process to an end.

It sounds potentially as if it's one of those things that could repeat itself. It's happened more than once; it's happened twice. So it could happen a third time.

Let's see if we can go on that journey of discovery to see what message is there, and understand what the 'karma tie' is wanting to fulfil, because it's there for a reason, isn't it? It's doing something. You know consciously you should break it, but there's an energy in it. There's a purpose in it. Let's see what we can find.

What we'll do is go through the process of relaxation. We'll go into the trance work, and I'll guide you all the way through it. Let's see what comes up. Okay?

Prea: Okay.

Therapist: Good. Do you have any questions for me?

Prea: No.

At this stage, the hypnotic induction was induced, followed by the trance deepeners and regression bridge – back into a past life.

Therapist: And there . . . you're there back in that life, that place, from some other time in some other place. Back there, you look down, and as you look down, you look at your feet. As you look at your feet, you feel what's on your feet, too. You're noticing maybe possible sounds around you. But you look at your feet. You notice what's on them. As you notice what's on them, I want you to tell me what you see there. What is it you notice?

Prea: Bare feet.

Therapist: Bare feet. I want you just to look and begin to move from your feet up to your ankles, and up to your calves and your shins, and what do you notice there?

Prea: A long skirt.

Therapist: It's a long skirt. And you follow the skirt up. What colour is the skirt?

Prea: It's white.

Therapist: What kind of material is it?

Prea: It's like cotton.

Therapist: A white cottony sort of material. You follow it up to your body. What do you notice on your body?

Prea: It's long, and it's covering me.

Therapist: It's long, and it's covering you. You move up, and I want you just to imagine that you hold your hands out in front of you. How do your hands look?

Prea: Small.

Therapist: Small. Feel yourself breathing, and then, I want you to imagine that you take your hands, and you move them up to your face and you touch your face. How does your face feel?

Prea: Soft and young.

Therapist: Then touch your hair. What's your hair like?

Prea: It's long. It's long and quite straight.

Therapist: It's long, and it's quite straight. You begin to get a sense as you feel your hair and your skin. And you feel your youngness. What kind of age are you? What number is that?

Prea: Eighteen, nineteen, eighteen, nineteen. I don't know.

Therapist: Okay. I want you to notice in that place. Where are you? What do you see around you in your immediate area?

Prea: It's a courtyard. There are houses made of wood.

Therapist: It's a courtyard with houses made of wood.

Prea: Yes. It's tied.

Therapist: They were tied together. They are tied together. Are you alone or is there anybody else there?

Prea: There's some people.

Therapist: There's some people there. Okay. I want you to look at the people. I want you to notice how they look. How many of them are there?

Prea: There's probably two over there, and some over there.

Therapist: Okay, and what are they doing?

Prea: Putting things into some carts. They are very busy.

Therapist: Okay, they're just busying themselves, they've got some carts, and they are just busy. Okay, so you're noticing them, you're noticing the wood, how it's tied. As you look around and you feel yourself moving and you feel your age about eighteen or nineteen.

Prea: Yes.

Therapist: Are you male or female?

Prea: Female.

Therapist: Female. What are you doing there?

Prea: I'm waiting.

Therapist: You're waiting. What are you waiting for?

Prea: Waiting for them to come back.

Therapist: And who is them?

Prea: My soldiers.

Therapist: Your soldiers.

Prea: Yes.

Therapist: You're waiting for the soldiers to come back. And, where are they?

Prea:	I don't know.
Therapist:	Are you a soldier?
Prea:	No.
Therapist:	You're not. What are you?
Prea:	I'm a wife, I'm his wife.
Therapist:	You're a wife.
Prea:	Yes.
Therapist:	You're the wife of one of the soldiers and you're waiting for them to come back. Where have they gone?
Prea:	I don't know. They go on their horses.
Therapist:	They go on their horses.
Prea:	Yes, they go for a long time.
Therapist:	And, this waiting, this waiting, and waiting, what's it like?
Prea:	It's lonely.
Therapist:	It's lonely. What do you really want?
Prea:	I just want them to come back.
Therapist:	When they come back, it sounds like it will make such a difference. What will be the difference?
Prea:	I won't be lonely.
Therapist:	You won't be lonely.
Prea:	Yes, there's nothing for me to do at the moment.
Therapist:	There's nothing for you to do, you're just lonely.
Prea:	It's such a wait.
Therapist:	Wait. All that waiting, and waiting. As you look around and you know why you're there, and you

know what you're doing, what else do you notice there?

Prea: It's quite cold and it's winter.

Therapist: Yes. Can you see anything else?

Prea: There's gates but we can't see out the gates until the gates are open.

Therapist: Yes. You're not able to see out?

Prea: No.

Therapist: What stops you?

Prea: I live in this place.

Therapist: You live in this place. What's that like living here?

Prea: There's nothing to do.

Therapist: You really want something to do?

Prea: Yes.

Therapist: What would you like to do?

Prea: Just leave.

Therapist: Yes. When you leave, where would you go?

Prea: I don't know.

Therapist: You really want to leave but you don't know where you'd go, just not there.

Prea: Because I don't know anywhere, just this place.

Therapist: When you just feel like yearning to go somewhere when not knowing what that is, because this is the only place you know. You've seen past the gates? Do you know what's out there?

Prea: Yeah.

Therapist: Yes? What is there?

Prea: There's just countryside.

Therapist: Just countryside.

Prea: Yes.

The therapist makes the decision, having established the scene with the client able to describe what they are experiencing, to move the experience a little further forward in time . . .

Therapist: Okay. Now, there. I want you to start noticing as time begins to move, just like that, moving throughout your body and time just moves. Beginning to move in a different direction than previously, moving just a little forward in time and keep moving just a little bit forward in time. As you move forwards in time, very soon finding yourself forward in time, on the count of three, one, and two, and three [*snaps fingers*]. Where are you in your life there?

Prea: Now, they've come back.

Therapist: They've come back. How is that?

Prea: It's a celebration.

Therapist: Do you feel like celebrating? How about you?

Prea: I'm just there.

Therapist: You're not celebrating?

Prea: It's not really allowed.

Therapist: It's not allowed? Who doesn't allow it?

Prea: The men.

Therapist: The same men.

Prea: Yes.

Therapist: What are you meant to do?

Prea: Just be there.

Therapist: Kind of the same as before then?

Prea: Yes.

Therapist: So they're back but really much hasn't changed.

Prea: No.

Therapist: And what's that like?

Prea: I'm glad he's back.

Therapist: And who is he?

Prea: He's my husband.

Therapist: What is his name?

Prea: I don't know.

Therapist: What does he look like?

Prea: He's quite . . . he's got light hair, and a beard.

Therapist: Yes. And you've seen him. He's been back to see you.

Prea: Yes.

Therapist: And how is that?

Prea: It's good.

Therapist: Okay. What are you doing there next?

Prea: I need to prepare the food.

Therapist: What's it like knowing that that's your next task?

Prea: That's wives' . . . that's what we do.

Therapist: Okay. And so just begin . . . just move with that. We're going to move again and just with that time I'm moving forwards even a little more. I'm moving forwards a little more. I'm moving forwards with time next. Moving to the next one, two, three, [*snaps fingers*], and where are you there?

Prea: I'm in a room.

Therapist: You're in a room. What's happening in that room?

Prea: I have a baby.

Therapist: You have a baby?

Prea: Yes.

Therapist: Boy or girl?

Prea: It's a girl.

Therapist: And what's her name?

Prea: I don't know.

Therapist: You don't know. As you're in that room you get a sense of the era that you're in. Maybe even a number comes to you of the year. Whatever number comes just let it come out.

Prea: 11 something. [*twelfth century*]

Therapist: 11 something. You're in the room with your baby. What are you doing there?

Prea: I'm tending the baby.

Therapist: You're tending the baby. And how's that?

Prea: It's good. We're playing.

Therapist: You're playing. What's it like?

Prea: It's nice. I like being with the baby. It gives me something to do.

Therapist: It gives you something to do, and that's really important.

Prea: Yes.

Therapist: You're a mother there. There's something to do.

Prea: The room is nice. It's warmer.

Therapist: It's a warmer room.

Prea: And it's nicer.

Therapist: Okay. What happens there?

Prea: There's more people around. There's more people there. It's better now.

Therapist: It's better. What's made it better?

Prea: I don't feel so sad.

Therapist: What stops you from feeling so sad?

Prea: It's the baby.

Therapist: You have the baby. And so what does that mean?

Prea: I'm not on my own.

Therapist: You're not on your own . . . but for years you're on your own, waiting, just waiting and waiting.

Prea: Yes.

Therapist: Now you have someone there relying on you. And then just moving and just flowing with that and moving forwards. Moving forwards with three . . . one, two, three [*snaps fingers*]. Where are you there?

Prea: It's the same place, it's still a fort. This is where we are left. There's some problems and trouble now.

Therapist: There's some problems and trouble. There's trouble now. They are coming.

Therapist: They are coming. Who's coming?

Prea: I don't know. The people.

Therapist: You don't know, more soldiers, or . . .

Prea: Yeah.

Therapist: And what does it feel like there?

Prea: I'm scared.

Therapist: You're scared. And what happens then?

Prea: We have to stop them coming. They can't come in.

Therapist: They can't come through that gate. And what will happen if they do?

Prea: They will kill us.

Therapist: And then what happens next?

Prea: The men have gone.

Therapist: And where have they gone?

Prea: I don't know. They left us.

Therapist: They've left you, how? They've left you. They've all gone and left . . . are there people still coming?

Prea: Yes.

Therapist: They're coming to get through that gate and the men have gone and left.

Prea: I don't know where the baby is.

Even though Prea becomes overwhelmed with emotion at this stage, it is vital to keep going.

Therapist: You don't know where the baby is. Where was the last time?

Prea: She was in the room.

Therapist: Where is she now?

Prea: I don't know. Someone's taken her.

Therapist: Who's taken her?

Prea: I don't know who's with her. A woman.

Therapist: One of the women? Which women?

Prea: I don't know . . . the women that look after the babies.

Therapist: Okay. What happens next?

Prea: They burn the fort.

Therapist: They burn. And where are you?

Prea: I don't know what to do.

Therapist: Okay. You don't know what to do, you're in there and it's burning. What are you thinking about that? What are your thoughts? What are you thinking?

Prea: I want to find the baby.

Therapist: You want to find the baby . . . and you can't.

Prea: No.

Therapist: What happens then?

Prea: My husband comes back.

Therapist: Where has he been?

Prea: He's been fighting.

Therapist: He's been fighting, and he's back . . . and what does he do then?

Prea: I think he's come for me but he doesn't . . . he has to go again.

Therapist: Yes. He has come back and he has to go again and now you're on your own again.

Prea: Yes.

Therapist: What are you going to do?

Prea: I don't know.

Therapist: What do you do next?

Prea: I'm so cross and angry. He doesn't seem to worry about us too much.

Therapist: You're just left there. Waiting again? Wondering.

Prea: It's not safe. It's not safe at all.

Therapist: Okay. And moving and flowing with that, forwards again even further and forwards again and one, two, three, [*snaps fingers*]. What's happening there?

Prea: It's sort of over . . . and it's over really.

There is a change in Prea's tone of voice, and she appears to have moved out of the traumatic experience.

Therapist: What's over?

Prea: The battle . . . everything is over.

Therapist: Yes, and you? Where are you?

Prea: I don't know where I am.

Therapist: What do you notice around you?

Prea: It's calm.

Therapist: It's calm. Where are you?

Prea: I don't know.

Therapist: What do you see?

Prea: There's nothing much to see.

Therapist: What do you hear?

Prea: It's just calm.

Therapist: Where are you?

Prea: I think I'm dead!

At this point, which appears to be the death experience, it is important to move the process back, to a few moments before, so we can get a sense of how the death came about.

Therapist: Okay. So you're now going to move time, back through time, back through time, and I want you to go back through time, back to just before that happened. One, two, three [*snaps fingers*], with your final moments before you were in that place, the end of that life. Where are you?

Prea: In the fort.

Therapist: In the fort. What's your age?

Prea: Twenty something.

Therapist: Twenty something. And what's happening around you?

Prea: They are fighting.

Therapist: Fighting again. This is just about to come to an end. I want you to just become aware of what thoughts you're having this time. It's happening again, isn't it? They're coming. What are the thoughts you're left with? What are the feelings that you're carrying because they're there, right at this final stage?

Prea: There's no one to protect us.

Therapist: There's no one to protect us. And how does it feel?

Prea: Just left, abandoned. No one cares.

Therapist: And you just allow the ending to happen. I want you to just allow the ending to happen and find yourself very soon back in the calm place . . . where nothing really much is happening.

Prea seemingly moves out of the experience and into this calm place . . .

Therapist: What colours are around you?

Prea: It's white.

Therapist: White. I want you just to follow the white. I want you to follow the white as it begins to shrink down. You see that? [*she nods*] Follow the white as it shrinks down and just getting closer and closer to the white. Ten, getting closer and closer. Nine, getting closer, eight and seven. We're going to go to that white light back into this life and six, five, and four and three and two and one. And . . . [*snaps fingers*] back into, back into this life, into that womb from where you started. Feel it . . . what do you hear?

Prea: Heartbeat.

Therapist: How do you feel?

Prea: Warm.

Therapist: Warm. I want you just very soon to become aware of what happens next and just moving forwards through time, and forwards through time and one, two, three [*snaps fingers*]. What's happening there?

Prea: I've been born.

Therapist: How do you know?

Prea: Because it's light.

Therapist: Because it's light and bright. I want you just to feel that very particular feeling and keep it that just been born feeling. Keep it, like you just grab hold of it with both hands. And you're keeping it safe. And just beginning to move forwards through time. As I count from one up to ten, you move up through time. One, moving you further forwards through the ages. Your current ages in this life, moving two, and three, and four, getting older. And five, getting older and bigger. And six, older and bigger. And seven, older, bigger, more grown up. And eight, moving right the way back and very soon to your current age. And nine, right the way back, just moving rapidly back now to your current age. And ten [*snaps fingers*] back to your current age today. And now, the now and today, take a nice deep breath. Just letting your eyes open.

Now we move into the 'processing' part of the session and explore what the experience was like for Prea and what she has discovered.

Prea: Wow! Thank you. That was pretty full on, wasn't it! Okay.

Therapist: Wow, yeah. Indeed. How are you feeling? What are you left with? I want to ask you questions but they're my questions. I want to know what you're feeling, where you're at.

Prea: You know, it kind of makes a lot of sense!

Therapist: Okay. So, tell us what makes sense and how.

Prea: I have this real thing about guys leaving me. I can't seem to get over that like I feel most people can, but I feel like really mortified by it.

Therapist: Really, what do you feel like when they've left?

Prea: Like left, yeah, like it's like a sense of indignance almost.

Therapist: Like they've left again, leaving you unsafe in a way.

Prea: Yeah. And I've never wanted children in this lifetime. I've never wanted a baby and I've never understood why I've never wanted a baby.

Therapist: What about now? Do you have a sense of now, understanding more about that?

Prea: Yeah! Because I was distraught like I couldn't find this baby. I think it had been killed . . . and I think he [*the husband*] hadn't come back because he'd been killed. I don't know. It's just like, "Wow!" So much dying and killing. And the other thing is the boredom, the complete boredom of not having anything to do. I was just like, you know, because in that time, there was . . . it wasn't like now where you could have careers and you would just, you know, there was just nothing to do.

Therapist: Yeah, there was nothing to read. There was no TV. There was no iPads or Google or internet, nothing to do.

Prea: There was nothing. None of the other people interacted with me because I was just the wife of this guy. I think he was quite a high-up guy.

Therapist: Right.

Prea: And I was just his wife and I was just hanging about doing nothing.

Therapist: And this is basically what happened, right? This is all there was to do.

Prea: Yeah. I didn't imagine it was that tedious. I mean, it's so funny because I have this thing about boredom as well. I have to, you know, I cannot stand being stuck and bored and feel like I'm not doing anything.

Therapist: Yeah.

Prea: It's really interesting though.

Therapist: Yeah, okay. Well, you've related it in a couple of areas to your life now. I guess I don't even need to ask you the (exploratory) questions really because it seems like those two very prominent things about being left and about a child. What about boredom, though? Because that seemed like a really prominent theme. What about your life now? What about boredom?

Prea: I don't allow myself to be bored really. I tend to drive myself to have new experiences, learn new things, do new things. I want to . . . you know, fill my life with good stuff.

Therapist: Yeah.

Prea: I can't be idle. I mean, I can relax and things but if it's long periods of inactivity, I can't cope with that.

Therapist: It's answered some questions . . . to some quite major areas of your life, to relationships, children, what you do with your time.

Prea: Yeah.

Therapist: Because it sounds like in that life, maybe [*the year*] 11 . . . something, whatever it was in that place, there was nothing to do. And you being left . . .

Prea: And you had no status also, that was the other thing. And I have a kind of, you know, need to be acknowledged a lot as well. And it's like you didn't exist. You were just this, you were just a wife, a female. It was like you were somebody's property and that's what it felt like.

Therapist: Right.

Prea: And yeah, that's another thing.

Therapist: This was a really powerful process. But what really powerfully happens in past life regression is the re-experiencing, the revivification . . . as if you were there and feeling yourself as if you were there once again. Not like you're remembering it or imagining it, it was more powerful then, yes?

Prea: Yeah. It's like when you visualise, you can sort of see, it's like you're disassociated but you're really associated with this. You're like *in* it.

Therapist: Yeah.

Prea: And that's the thing, you can't come out of it either. You know, you can't sort of pull back. It seems like you're gripped into that moment. You know . . . it's quite unusual.

Therapist: There's something connecting maybe a few dots for you there . . . about letting go of these links and . . .

Prea: And expectations, thinking that people have to look after you. That's another one.

Therapist: Right. I already want to ask you the question now. Do you think it will be easier to do that?

Prea: I hope so, now I understand it.

Therapist: Do you think it will?

Prea: I hope so.

Therapist: Alright. It needs some time.

Prea: Yeah. I'll let you know.

Therapist: Hey, brilliant.

Prea: Thank you so much.

Therapist: Thank *you* so much.

Session Feedback

It may be enlightening at this stage to revisit Prea's account of this session from the Chapter 1, as whilst we could read many meanings into her story, the only feedback of importance is Prea's personal experience.

Here again are Prea's reflections, around three months on from her past life regression experience.

> "The life that I was being shown was strangely paralleling aspects of my current life experience. At the time of the regression, I was in a relationship that seemed to mirror some aspects of the life that I saw during the PLTT. My present relationship had a strange connection and familiarity

that I had not experienced in previous relationships. Also, it was a very difficult relationship that triggered profound insecurities and anxiety, which was destroying it.

The more we tried to break away from each other, the harder it was to let go of each other. There was a mutual sense of unfinished business between us, which was very uncomfortable. The PLTT showed me what my life had been like within this relationship in a previous lifetime. The events surrounding my death in that life seemed to have been carried forward in my psyche in this lifetime.

I had been shown some information during the PLTT, so I followed it up with some research. I had a date and location along with clear imagery of the buildings, how they were constructed and so on. What I found out was astonishing.

I found art work from that era depicting battle scenes similar to what I saw in the regression. I found historical information describing a feudal waring society circa 1200. I had a sense of myself wearing a white dress and I found a similar type of outfit and hair style in my researching that I had experienced in the PLTT.

This was really strange, but even stranger was a conversation that I had with my partner following the regression. I explained my experience of our relationship during the regression, how I had died alone, waiting for him to return. He then told me that he had visited a psychic, a woman who had recounted a past life to him. She had told him that she had died in medieval Japan after a battle, when she was a small child. She told him that she had a clear memory of the events, described hiding throughout the battle and then finding her mother lying dead in a pool of blood. She described sitting with her mother's body waiting for her father to return and eventually starved to death. She had told him that he had been her father in that previous lifetime and that she knew they would meet in this lifetime.

What I found fascinating was that she could not have known my own past life experience prior to her revealing this to my partner. I had not even discussed the child part of my regression experience with him. This additional information was coming from a third party and it answered my question of what had happened to the child. During the regression, I was deeply distressed about not knowing where the child was during the battle but now I had my answer.

The regression has changed me profoundly. I had always carried a deep and inexplicable sadness, which I have been conscious of for most of my life. After the regression, I felt an almost instant release from the sadness, I felt that a heaviness had lifted from my heart. As time has gone by I have felt more confident, calmer and more at ease with the world. I no longer feel worried about things that I can't control and am less anxious about outcomes.

I have been able to finally find closure with my ex-partner and we have worked on our separation respectfully, without either of us holding onto any destructive residual emotions. I am convinced that these changes have arisen from being able to contextualise (what I believe to be) a deep and ancient memory that has been tapping me on the shoulder for most of my life.

From my experience during the PLTT, I have been shown the source of these residual emotions and I no longer feel compelled to re-live this experience. I have been able to release this and free myself."

A powerful experience indeed. Let's move then into the next important stage of entering the spirit realm and find out exactly what needs to be done there and how we do this.

Chapter 10
Past Life Transpersonal Therapy
The Transformational Realm

Just as a candle cannot burn without fire,
men cannot live without a spiritual life.
Buddha

Ready for the Next Steps

So far, you have guided the person through the regression process, entered the past life, explored it, and garnered the details. Then you moved them through to the death transition, finding out what thoughts they took with them at the end of their life and what unfinished business they were left with. Let's now add the final steps that complete the process.

The Full PLTT Process

To this point, you have completed steps one to five, so it's time to move to the spirit realm in order to gain learning from the spirit guides, deal with any unfinished business with one or more people in the past life, and make the body choice for the next life. Here we enter into the dialoguing process where learning from the past life can be relayed forward to the next life, and the incarnation of that life can gain clarity over their life to come. We then move from the spirit realm to the next life, until finally returning to the present life, at which stage we then explore what has been learned and what meanings have been unearthed. Here is the full nine step process:

1. The hypnotic induction and regression techniques specific to Past Life Transpersonal Therapy.
2. Embodiment of the past life character. Keeping in the 'past-present' tense and in the past life body.
3. Establishing the scene in detail: Where are you? Who else is there? What do you see? When is this? What year? What else?
4. Exploring the past life. How the life is lived and develops, examining poignant moments.
5. Moving to the moment of death and discovery of what's taken through to the death transition.
6. Transcending to the spirit realm.
7. Learning within the spirit realm through confrontation
8. Meeting and learning from the spirit guides.
9. The next life body choice.
10. Future-self dialoguing process.
11. Moving from the spirit realm to the next (or current) life.
12. Integration into this life and the learning exploration.

THE SPIRIT REALM

In Buddhism, the spirit realm is a place referred to as the Bardo of Becoming. It is where the past incarnation is looked back upon, the wisdom from the spirit guides is encountered, and choices are made about the next incarnation, guided by the soul and the karmic message. This place is "The mental gateway into the spirit world" (Newton, 2004, p. 63), and it is here that much of the explicit healing takes place. In the spirit realm, we can specifically encounter a holding ground, a dedicated place for learning and healing. Here we are able to focus on pursuits such as encountering, dialoguing, embodiment, choice, learning, and transformation, as well as the fundamental questions of life – such as Tomlinson (2006, p. 96) suggests, "Who am I?" and "Why am I here?"

In the last chapter, Prea moved directly to the white light, moving to her present-day life. Her learning at this time was complete. In practical terms, however, after the experience of the moment of death, you would normally suggest that they move up out of their body, into the air, seeing themselves back on earth getting smaller and smaller, seeing the land, and oceans beneath them . . . getting higher through the atmosphere, seeing the earth beneath them . . . feeling space and the universe all around them. As they connect with the universal energy, they eventually settle themselves in the spirit realm.

Once in the spirit realm, there are four stages to the healing process that happen:

1. Confrontation.
2. Meeting the spirit guides.
3. Choosing the next body form.
4. Dialoguing with the future self.

Confrontation

In the confrontation phase there is the opportunity to meet the problematic person or persons in that life. This is perhaps someone who did you great wrongs, or who was absent, or who stopped you doing something that you were meant to do. Whoever this might be, you need to engage in a dialogue. There are important things you have to say to them and learnings to gain. Let's look at some past life characters you may come across in the confrontation. We've witnessed a child reunited with one of his lost parents; a slave who needed to confront the slave owner; a younger brother who confronted an older brother for bullying him and leaving him destitute; and a wife encountering her husband and his infidelity.

You may even need to confront someone that you yourself have wronged to explain your side of things and to make amends. There are many different scenarios in which conflict may have arisen. The conflict needs resolving, and that resolution comes through the dialoguing process.

Here is a question we want you to think about and explore, and record your thoughts in relation to what comes up for you. If you came back to your current life from a future incarnation of you, who do you think would be the object of your confrontation? Where would you find there has been no resolution? Think of this as your unfinished business or one of those open loops.

If you have a conflict with another person in your life that you've been unable to resolve, there will be something happening at a deeper level than your conscious mind knows. This is where past life therapy can really help. Who is this person and what is unresolved?

Most of the time the unfinished business is a relationship problem. It could be directly about someone else or about the fact that there was no one else, and life was lonely and isolated. Or it could be about your perception of someone else, their perception of you, or what you think they perceived about you.

Often this stage of the healing process can unearth some difficult feelings, as for many people confrontation is something to be avoided at all costs. If this resonates with you, then you might find yourself shying away from confronting an issue that really should be addressed, avoiding certain people or tasks because they are too stressful to face. This is mostly due to the fact that we can't predict where matters will end up. It's important to remember, however, that in this process we are in theta state where the critical factor is less engaged, making confrontation and resolution possible.

It is useful to see the confrontation in the spirit realm as a powerful opportunity for communication, and in the spirit realm you are guided and empowered through your spirit guides to use this opportunity of communication for healing at the highest level, as your soul and the soul of the other come together to create the reconciliation and peace that sets you *both* free. May (1972) writes, "Communication leads to community, that is, to understanding, intimacy and the mutual valuing that was previously lacking (pp. 246-247).

Something incredible can happen when two people actually talk to each other and listen to what the other person has to say. When they respectfully listen to and really hear each other the problem has space to get resolved. The same thing happens quite powerfully during the past life process because once you have identified the unfinished business, you are open to resolving this with whomever. A great example of this is shown in Maarja's session in the next chapter.

The process continues as follows:

As the facilitator you invite the person you're guiding through the regression to bring forward the problem individual(s) in the past life, the one(s) they are most in need of resolving something with, and then you ask them to confront what needs to be said. Encourage them to express themselves about what happened, how they feel about what happened, what they thought, what it left them with, as well as how it impacted them. Then you invite the other 'conflict' person to respond, to share their experience of the situation. You keep moving back and forth between the characters until you feel that enough has been said and that better clarity, understanding, and mutual appreciation has been achieved. This alters previously held perceptions, misunderstandings, and judgements, bringing harmony to what once niggled away in the background of your mind.

Meeting the Spirit Guides

In western spiritualism, a spirit guide is a non-physical entity who acts as a guide to a living, incarnated human being. Popular images of these are often portrayed as angels or guardian angels. Your spirit guides are always around you throughout each life you live, watching over you as you move through stages of your current existence. They emanate from the one true spirit that 'is'. Our spirit guides have a unique connection with our souls thus you might often sense them there beside you as you ask for help or when you call for strength in a moment of need. They are there listening; they have great understanding about your purpose and mission in life. In everyday life we most often connect to our spirit guides in some kind of 'spiritual emergency' (Grof and Grof, 1990; Friedman and Hartelius, 2015).

Your spirit guides help you be in the right place at the right time – some of which could be difficult or painful – so that you can live in alignment with your life goals and what you are here in this world to do, as well as what karma needs to be addressed. Do you know your spirit guides? You might be surprised to know that this could well be the case. As American author, James Van Praagh (2017) writes,

> Our guides occupy an infinite array of spiritual dimensions and may have never incarnated at all, or they can be family members and friends who we have known in this lifetime, and who have since made the transition to spirit. (p. 3)

In those difficult times when you feel you are being looked after by a loved one now departed from this world, it may well be them, their spiritual essence 'looking down on you', acting as your spirit guide to help you along your way.

In this stage of the process, you are able to meet your spirit guides and gain from their wisdom. They are able to convey the things you need to know in a much more explicit way, and in a way that will help you in your future journey to your next life. This could be in the form of a new perspective, an idea, corrections about beliefs you have of yourself, or corrections about beliefs you have of others or you think others have of you.

It's here you can really help people to find what they need to move forwards in their life so that they can embrace it with vibrancy. This is where a knowing comes from within their soul, with a deeper sense of what they are there for and who they are destined to be.

For you or the people you help using past life therapy, meeting the spirit guides is where the wisdom that is needed at this precise moment in time is gained. This clears the path for taking the next step.

The process continues as follows:

As the facilitator, you introduce the spirit guides into the process by suggesting to the person you're working with that you will count to three, snap your fingers, and then the spirit guides will begin to approach them. One, two, three [*snap*] . . . and ask them to bring their spirit guide or guides close so that they can describe them.

Tell them next that the spirit guide is the one who indeed has all the wisdom and knowledge about them and their life and holds all they need to know for their future lives. You then invite the spirit guide to speak or convey a message in any way that is appropriate, suggesting that all they need to do is listen and hear, and allow themselves to be open to the message their spirit guide is offering them.

Give time for the information to be absorbed, and then ask what the spirit guide has said, and invite a dialogue between them. This makes sure there is a full understanding and acceptance of what the spirit guide has presented, what has been heard, and what has been conveyed and said back in relation to that. It's important for them to convey the dialogue to you aloud and to repeat the spirit guide's words so that they can fully embed the meaning within their mind and body as they hear themselves.

This is frequently the reason why talking therapy works, not just past life therapy. When you speak of your concerns, worries, or struggles, and speak them out loud to another person who won't judge, condemn, criticise or advise you, you will begin to experience a more 'pure' essence of you. Your words can be heard by you, with no secrets, making it easier to revise what you mean so you become more aligned to your greater truth and thus your higher self.

The next question to consider, is if your spirit guides could help you with something that you are really struggling with or something that you just can't tolerate (or have never been able to tolerate), what would it be and how do you imagine they could possibly help you at this point?

YOUR BODY CHOICE

Once the spirit guides have imparted their wisdom through the dialoguing, the learning has been enabled and is ready to be carried through to the next life within karma. The next part of this process involves the incarnation of the future life body, which means that you need to choose your next bodily form. Then the dialogue continues, this time between your soul and your future life self. This will connect the learning through to your next existence and inform the future life self the karmic message being carried forward.

For most people, selecting their next life body is a powerful experience. This comes as no surprise when you consider the intrinsic role of your body in the experience of being human. As French phenomenological philosopher Maurice Merleau-Ponty (1945/2002) describes, the body is "a power of natural expression" (p. 211). He sees it as the origin of expressive movement, which impacts one's actions and perceptions of the world. It is through the body that we have access to the world. Meaning is lived through bodily experience and action, and "emotions use the body as their theatre" (Damasio, 2000, p. 51). Indeed Merleau-Ponty further sums up the entwined nature of our body in our experiencing of living, "Our own body is in the world as the heart is in the organism" (p. 203).

Consider for a moment that in your previous life's incarnation, in the spirit realm, you chose the body you're in right now. To think about your body in this way might be a rather frustrating or upsetting proposition, especially if you are experiencing bodily illness or pain. If you think about the notion that from your previous life, you stepped into this body and you chose it, it may well bring up a lot for you to consider. That's quite a powerful prospect, but it can also be a great source of healing.

Bearing that in mind, what we'd like you to do now is think about the decision taken in the spirit realm for your present-day body. Look deeper into the choice you made in relation to what it might mean. The soul knows in advance the karmic lesson to be faced and chooses the body accordingly.

Describe your present body. What do you feel you carry in it? And in what way does it inform you about the possible messages you need to hear? For example, do you feel you have a strong body that has been able to tolerate stress and some neglect? Or perhaps you have a body susceptible to illness, which compels you to divert your concentration towards a more spiritual path?

In terms of your previous life body choice, there is an important reason you chose the body you inhabit today. As Newton (2004, p. 176) writes, "Souls seem to know which body would be their best choice for learning and they usually choose it." The body is chosen to enable the karmic message to come to light, and so the ease or difficulty of being in the body you reside in today holds some message for your present life.

In the spirit realm you'll be given a number of body choices. Newton describes that this usually ranges from between two to five, and that there is most often a 'leading candidate' (2004, p. 176). In our experience, once the spirit guides have imparted their wisdom, the learning of the next life has already begun, and the body choice process is already under way. In this manner, the leading candidate presents itself strongly as the choice of body for your next incarnation.

However, bear in mind that an exploration of the potential bodies presenting themselves as possible vessels for incarnation in the next life is a useful process to move through, as we have often heard clients describe that they believe they were born into the wrong body. Whilst it may be that the choice is indicative of the karmic learning necessary, an exploration of each potential body choice can shed light on the deeper possible reasoning of the final body choice that is made.

The next part is to try on for size each of the bodies presented as a possible choice. How does it fit? What does it feel like? How does it move? What does each body offer? What do you notice about that body? What might be your mission in that body? Take some time to explore each potential choice, until the final body choice is found. Once that choice has been made, you can move on to the next stage, the dialoguing process.

From Life-to-Life – Dialoguing with the Body to Be

The next stage of the flow of learning from life-to-life is further dialoguing. This is the most important part of the process when connecting what happens in one life to the next. You begin then, within the spirit realm, to guide the dialogue between the soul and the future, soon-to-be-born incarnation – their body to be.

The process continues as follows:

From the spirit realm, you guide them to see themselves reaching out to touch the chosen body of their future self. They hold that body's face or hand tenderly, feel their future body's skin, look into their eyes, and smell their scent. Suggest that they can begin to recognise that they are the sole source in all existence that can actually tell their future self what it needs to hear right now.

Guide them to tell their future self what will most help them live a life of alignment in accordance with the message and spirit of karma, as well as what will best enable them to live in harmony with their purpose and life mission. In this they help their future self know that whatever happens in their life, it is part of their divine passage through eternal time in just the way it is meant to be. Then ask that they become quiet and listen. After a short time, you suggest they imagine switching places with their future 'self to be' who has just heard this message, and then ask the questions that allow for further exploration and understanding: "What would you like to say back in response to what you've heard?" "How do you feel about the learnings that have been conveyed to you?" "What do you make of 'who' you are?" and "How does it feel to know the purpose of your being?"

You ask them then to return to their soul, having heard what their future incarnation has just conveyed and ask them if they have any further insights or wisdom that their future life self could benefit from hearing. If they do, then now is the time to pass on that information.

The objective of this dialogue, which we continue until there is a sense of clarity, is transparency. When all is out in the open, a sense of relief tends to be experienced as we know where we stand and can then more assuredly assess where we go next.

Moving into Further Past Lives

Having chosen the next body to be and engaged in the dialogue that passes over the karmic message and learning from the spirit realm, it is time to enter the next life. The soul enters the body-to-be, to join as one.

In essence, this next part of the process is a reversal of the regression process. From the spirit realm we then re-enact the regression visualisation of looking for the light, only this time the light leads to the next incarnation's life, into the womb of the mother of their future life, into the being they have just dialogued with.

Once you have guided the rebirth and they have arrived in the next life, you then begin to explore that incarnation as before, starting at step two of the Past Life Transpersonal Therapy process, the embodiment of the character (see Chapter 8). Moving them through each of the steps again, enables the learning from several past lives in any one session. Each time you will discover the journey of karma and which aspects of your past lives have either been fulfilled or which you still carry within you as part of your current life's essential learning.

BACK INTO THE PRESENT

At some stage of this process, it will become appropriate to return to the current life experience, in order to make sense of the messages and learnings gained from the past life explorations. This may well happen as part of the movement from the past life to the next, the next being *this* current life (as with Prea). We suggest that two past lives are the maximum for someone to process in one session. If you travel through more past lives than this, then there will likely be too much information to work with therapeutically in the processing phase of the experience.

Therefore, although choosing the next body in the spirit realm can happen naturally, there will be times when you may specifically need to guide this process to the current life incarnation. At the 'body choice' step, you ask them to choose the body they have now. Then, once you have created the dialogue between the soul and the body to be, ask them to find and follow the light back into the womb of their present-day mother.

Once the rebirthing has taken place, you can then offer them suggestions of growing back up to their current age. They need to return to the present-day body, sense of self, and surroundings.

Once the chronological age has been reached and they have opened their eyes, we begin the final phase of processing the experience.

Being There in Spirit – The Processing

This is crucial to the therapeutic aspect of the work. Once back into the present there is a need to know the various meanings of what has been experienced and to find out what they have gained from this. This is where the opportunity arises to truly integrate the learning into the now, enabling the sharing of their experience with conscious awareness. They can then begin to link their past life or lives to their possible present life's challenges. For many of the people we've worked with, the struggles they are experiencing make perfect sense at this stage. However, there is a need to formulate this into words.

What questions do you ask here? Well, at this point we want to elicit as much understanding as possible. It's important to remember that the past life or lives have been experienced by your client in an altered state of consciousness and so becoming aware of their journey at a fully conscious level will increase their awareness of the meanings behind that experience. Let them talk. Be curious and explore.

As you did with the earlier stages of the process, you can use both open and closed questions to help them elucidate what happened, with the focus on exploring what has been learned and what has been healed. This brings us closer to understanding what French artist Paul Gauguin titled his 1897 painting, 'Where Do We Come From? What Are We? Where Are We Going?'

In the next chapter, we'll see how the whole process unfolds as you follow the transcripts of two further Past Life Transpersonal Therapy experiences.

Chapter 11
In Action
Healing within the Past Life Spirit Realm

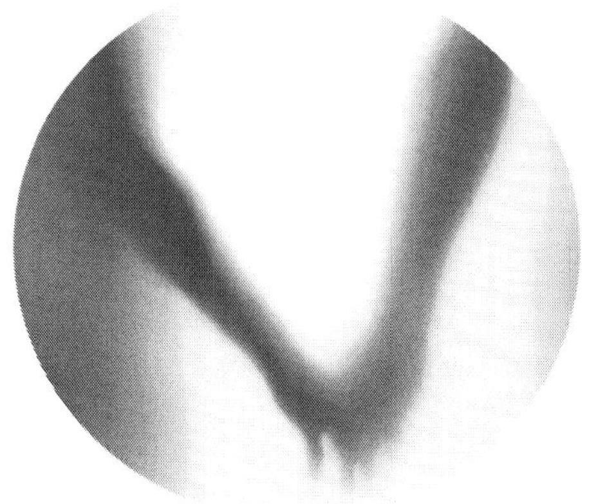

You were born a child of light's wonderful secret,
you return to the beauty you have always been.
Aberjhani, *Visions of a Skylark Dressed in Black*

Introduction

We begin this chapter with a demonstration session from one of our Past Life Transpersonal Therapy workshops. This session demonstrates the full PLTT process from start to finish.

Maarja's Past Life Session

In this session, Maarja describes how a previous relationship was impinging on her current relationship, stopping her from living her life in the way she wanted: connected and present.

Maarja: In my life there is my husband, and my ex-partner. Every single time when my relationship with my husband becomes a bit stuck, my ex-partner comes into my mind and into the picture. I have tried to limit these thoughts but it's not working. I've expressed all the feelings I have towards my ex-partner . . . but every time I come to the city for work, in the back of my head I have an idea that maybe we will meet up. My mind is telling me that I have a great relationship at home and I say to myself, "but what are you missing, woman . . . come on!" And then I wonder what my ex-partner is doing and I then get mad with myself.

Therapist: So tell me what's so difficult about this?

Maarja: It's difficult for me because I feel I am tearing up from the inside. I'm wondering what it is about him that makes me think about him and feel about him in this way. Oh . . . I also need to add that he is the father of my child.

Therapist: I see, so you can't just forget him.

Maarja: No.

Therapist: Because he is going to be some part of your life for as long as you have a child together.

Maarja: As a parent I understand that because we have a child for our entire lives . . . this part is clear, this is how it is and it's fine. But what is disturbing is how I feel when we meet . . . the sensations in my body when we meet . . . it is like we are melting. It is also not only this passion when we meet . . . it is also that when he hugs me and he holds me strongly it feels perfect and I could spend three days like that. I could cry because I would like to not have these feelings.

Therapist: So what are the feelings?

Maarja: I don't know how to describe these feelings but it is like he is living within me. And I feel like I am cheating within myself because I am living with my husband and while everything is very good . . . I would like to have our marriage without this third person around us.

Therapist: Do you get the sense that you can't let go of him?

Maarja: Something like that. There is something to learn, something I need to resolve . . . because we are separate, and we have let go. He has his own life and I have mine, there is nothing between us . . . and then what happens is that he shows up or I show up and then the avalanche of emotion all starts moving again.

Therapist: Are you saying that you don't want that anymore because you want that with your husband?

Maarja: Yes.

Therapist: So do you have that with him?

Maarja: This marriage is really safe, and I can be who I am in my marriage. I really don't know how I would compare them, but when my husband and I met the avalanche of emotion was there, yes. Maybe now we don't do so many things together. We have walked a long road together, but my side relationship with my ex has become public knowledge in our house. If I have to compare these two feelings of seeing my ex and being with my husband, then on the side of my husband it is warm and safe, and on the other hand with my ex it is insecure and passionate.

Therapist: Does this mean you are left with choosing between safety and passion?

Maarja: Yes.

Therapist: And is it difficult to make the choice?

Maarja: Yes, it is.

Therapist: So do you get a sense of what is stopping you from making the choice?

Maarja: Maybe it is about these old experiences because I have already lived together with my ex and there was nothing there that I have now in my marriage. But today if I got back into the boat with him then maybe it would still be the same. Maybe I am afraid.

Therapist: So you are searching for what this is about and you're imagining what it might be like to go back. And you can't quite find out what is stopping you making this choice. Is this right?

Maarja: Yes.

Therapist: So how about we look somewhere else . . . at what might be behind this.

Maarja: Yeah. Because I have this feeling . . . that what is happening in this life . . . these things that are taking place here . . . are not from here. Like something bigger has happened.

Therapist: Okay. So let's go exploring.

At this stage, the hypnotic induction was induced, followed by the trance deepeners and regression bridge – back into a past life.

Therapist: And so as you look down at your feet . . . what do you see?

Maarja: Green grass.

Therapist: So you are standing on green grass. What do you notice around you?

Maarja: A large field of grass.

Therapist: It's a large field of grass . . . and I want you now to look up at your legs and tell me what you notice.

Maarja: Comfortable shoes.

Therapist: And as you look up at your body? What are you wearing on your body?

Maarja: A woolen skirt.

Therapist: And I want you to reach out with one of your hands and just look at your hand and turn it over. How does it look?

Maarja: Graceful.

Therapist: Now I want you to reach out with the other hand and put them together. How do your hands feel?

Maarja: Silky.

Therapist: Take your hands and put them to your face. What's that like?

Maarja: Very soft.

Therapist: Okay, and what's happening around you there?

Maarja: There are sheep somewhere. I can hear the bells that the sheep are wearing.

Therapist: So you are in this green field and you can feel the silky softness of your skin and you can hear the sheep. What is your age?

Maarja: Thirty.

Therapist: And are you male or female?

Maarja: Female.

Therapist: What year is it?

Maarja: 1817.

Therapist: What is your name?

Maarja: Clara.

Therapist: What are you doing there, Clara?

Maarja: Looking towards a house that's there. I live in the house.

Therapist: Do you want to walk to the house?

Maarja: Yes.

Therapist: So as you begin to walk to the house and take each step and you look around you . . . you notice what else is there. What is happening around you?

Maarja: There are some trees in the distance and the sheep have grazed the grass and it looks very nice.

Therapist: And you keep walking . . . And I wonder if you notice where you are there . . . where is it?

Maarja: Ireland . . . or maybe England? It smells fresh.

Therapist: Okay. I want you to go to the house. And when you reach the house . . . then go inside. What do you notice? What's there?

Maarja: A dining room, a living room . . . a stairway. I go to the stairs and the first floor. There's a very warm light. It's extremely nice.

Therapist: Is there anyone else there or is it just you?

Maarja: Just me.

Therapist: So what I want you then to do . . . when I count to three and snap my fingers I want you to move a little forwards in time there . . . one, two, three [*snap*] . . . what's happening there?

Maarja: Same building, same place . . . I am in someone's room. And he is there.

Therapist: Do you know who that is? Do you know them? Who is it? . . . [*Maarja becomes emotional*] . . . keep breathing . . . Who is that?

Maarja: My companion. He is leaving.

Therapist: How does he look?

Maarja: Big.

Therapist: Big . . . and he is going . . . and do you know where he is going?

Maarja: He is leaving me [*Maarja becomes tearful*].

Therapist: Keep breathing . . . just keep breathing. He is leaving you?

Maarja: Yes, it seems so. We had an argument. He doesn't understand me. He says he feels a stranger in the house. He doesn't understand me.

Therapist: So he feels a stranger in the house . . . and he is leaving. And what's it like for you?

Maarja: Very painful.

Therapist: And what happens then?

Maarja: There is nothing that is helping. We are both there and in the manor house. But the house belongs to me and it's equally our house, but it doesn't seem that way to him.

Therapist: Because it is your house? [*Maarja nods*] . . . he can't accept it's your house. And so he is leaving?

Maarja: He doesn't want to go but it is as if he *has* to go.

Therapist: And what happens next?

Maarja: I am walking towards him and feel worried. There is nothing I can say to him. I want to make him stay . . . [*she cries*].

Therapist: But there is nothing you can do to make him stay . . . so what do you do then?

Maarja: He goes.

Therapist: And he goes. And there is nothing you can do to stop him. And so I want you to begin . . . as I count from one to three . . . just moving forwards in time . . . just keep moving forwards in time, in that place, in that life . . . getting older and older . . . until you reach the moment just before your death. One, two, three [*snap*] . . . Where are you there?

Maarja: Same house, black dress.

Therapist: And what is your age?

Maarja: Eighty-nine.

Therapist: Eighty-nine. And you begin to become aware of how life has been.

Maarja: Empty.

Therapist: And has it been empty since he left?

Maarja: Yes. Nothing has happened since he went.

Therapist: And now you are old and you are about to leave that place . . . you are about to move to another place. And you are now just a few moments before you take your last breath. And you become aware of the message you carry with you from that life . . . And the learnings that you have taken and what you are left with . . . and what is that?

Maarja: Why couldn't I have stopped him?

Therapist: And what else?

Maarja: It's been empty.

Therapist: It's been empty since he left?

Maarja: Yeah. Nothing has happened since he has left and now I am old.

Therapist: And now you are old and about to leave this place. To another place. And just a few moments before you take your last breath . . . you become aware of the messages you carry from this life. And the learnings that you have taken. And what you are left with . . . what is that?

Maarja: Why couldn't I have stopped him?

Therapist: And as you go forwards to take your last breath . . . how do you go now?

Maarja: I am waiting to go. Waiting.

Therapist: So you take your last breath and you find yourself drifting . . . just drifting up . . . and you start to find yourself . . . as you drift up and up . . . just being there within the spirit realm just drifting and floating . . . and how does it feel there?

Maarja: Everything is new. And I am looking for something.

Therapist: Just drifting . . . your soul . . . beginning to search . . . and you know what it is that you are looking for.

Maarja: Someone is waiting for me.

Therapist: But you are looking and looking for that someone, but they can't find you. Because something needs to happen. So as you drift in this place searching, I want to become aware of that person from that previous life . . . just appearing there within the spirit realm, because there is something unfinished there . . . something that needs to happen, that needs to be said to that person from the previous life . . . and as they appear in front of you tell me who they are.

Maarja: It is the same man but he is young. A boy.

Therapist: He is a little boy. What's that like?

Maarja: Warm.

Therapist: And as you see him as a little boy . . . I wonder what it is that you want to say to him. Things that were maybe left unsaid from that previous life because he wouldn't listen, because he couldn't hear. And you didn't understand. What might you like to say to him now?

Maarja: Sorry for acting as your mother did and not letting you be a man.

Therapist: And as you say that, what does he say back?

Maarja: He is looking at me wide-eyed . . . as if he doesn't believe me or understand me.

Therapist: So what more would you like to say that will help him understand? He is looking confused.

Maarja: I should bring him closer.

Therapist: So you bring him close to you and put your arms around him.

Maarja: He holds my hands now, and I want to tell him I love him.

Therapist: And you hold his hands . . . and you look into his eyes and you tell him you love him so much. How does he look?

Maarja: He looks sad . . . in his eyes. He feels sorry that he couldn't find the words.

Therapist: And as you hear he is sorry for not finding the words . . . how does it feel?

Maarja: It's an understanding.

Therapist: Is there anything else that you need to say to each other there?

Maarja: Just . . . I'm sorry.

Therapist: And as you say you're sorry, does he say anything back?

Maarja: He smiles and laughs . . . he is forgiving me.

Therapist: How does that feel?

Maarja: It feels good. He is letting me know we will return and meet again.

Therapist: What else . . . [*long pause*] what are you noticing.

Maarja: A release.

Therapist: A release. So with that release . . . what happens with him now?

Maarja: He is skipping off into the clouds.

Therapist: And how is that for you?

Maarja: I am sad that he has left, but I am glad. I want him to have his own experiences.

Therapist: So I want you then to just watch him as he skips off into the clouds. Off on his own journey, into eternity, into whatever next lives he chooses and experiences, and when you have let him go, he can go and live his own life . . . and so then you begin to move through the spirit realm . . . and then you come across your spirit guides . . . and from that process of letting go, they are now there to impart the wisdom that you need. Learnings that they have been carrying for eternity, waiting for you to arrive, to tell you what you really need to know . . . and to hear . . . as you get ready for the next life. And the spirit guides present themselves before you and tell you what you need to hear. And you just listen . . . and as you listen and hear what they are saying . . . what is it that you hear?

Maarja: Be honest . . . hold on to your wisdom.

Therapist: Be honest . . . hold on to your wisdom . . . and what else?

Maarja: Be patient.

Therapist: Be honest . . . hold on to your wisdom and be patient.

Maarja: Everything happens at precisely the right time.

Therapist: Be honest . . . hold on to your wisdom, be patient . . . Everything happens precisely at the right moment . . . and you take those messages and those learnings . . . which are exactly the right learnings in this place, within the spirit realm . . . and your soul absorbs that . . . readying you for the next life . . . with that learning . . . and as you move within the spirit realm you come across your choices of body. There may be two or three choices . . . and just one of those bodies will appeal to you. It will be just the right body for you to carry that learning . . . into the next life. You might like to just move into that body and feel it . . . notice what it is like . . . and how does it feel?

Maarja: It's an old man with a long beard. He knows so many things and he is nice and comfortable.

Therapist: Okay . . . so do you choose that body?

Maarja: Yeah.

Therapist: Yes. So you get a sense of you and that future life in that body. And from within the spirit realm, from deep within your body you can tell that future you just what it needs to hear right now. You can impart that knowledge from that magical place, from the most powerful place of wisdom . . . to your future present-day self. What would you like to tell your future present-day self that would really help them, to live the life they choose? The life they *should* live?

Maarja: Trust the wisdom within.

Therapist: In a moment I am going to count from one to three and snap my fingers and when I do you will become that future self. One, two, three *[snap]* . . . and as that future self, having heard what that 'soul you' has said. Is there anything you would like to say back?

Maarja: Yes, I will share the wisdom within . . . I will be a teacher. Now I have the wisdom of an old man and I can share it with all my students.

Therapist: On the count of three I am going to snap my fingers and you will move back in to the spirit realm as the soul. One, two, three [*snap*] . . . And you have heard what that future self has said. Is there anything else that the future self needs to hear?

Maarja: Trust . . . 200 percent.

Therapist: And as you look at the future self and they hear that message, how do they look?

Maarja: He is giving a small nod.

Therapist: They have heard. And then you begin to move through the spirit realm, drifting and floating, drifting and floating . . . and then you will see that small light . . . that bright small light, and you reach out to it and you reach towards it . . . and slowly begin to move towards that light . . . the light back into this life . . . and you get closer and closer . . . closer and closer . . . and as I count from five to one you get closer and closer until I get to one . . . and you move into the light, five, four, three, two, moving right into the light, right through the light and one, back into this present-day life and beginning to be just aware of time and space, drifting back through time . . . back up . . . slowly growing up, back up to your present age, getting bigger and bigger, older and older, feeling the wisdom within permeating throughout every part of you . . . through your mind, body, and soul drifting right the way up . . . and on the count of three drifting back to this time and place . . . one, two, three, [*snap*] . . . eyes open, alert and aware.

Now we move into the 'processing' part of the session and explore what the experience was like for Maarja and what she has discovered.

Therapist: How are you?

Maarja: I have known everything we've explored, it's been somewhere within me for some time now, but knowing with an accompanying picture was profound. In being the body of the old man . . . it wasn't even a body . . . it was more like a being. It's like he is with me . . . but I have the courage to trust in it. It's like I have been looking for confirmation of my ideas from somewhere for some time . . . or proof of something, and now I have it. And knowing now that he lacked the vocabulary from within . . . it helps.

Therapist: And now?

Maarja: I don't know what now. It's better. A sense of release, it's hard to explain.

Therapist: Okay. Through this journey and this process, how has this illuminated what is happening in your life?

Maarja: If I really think about things, my ex-partner . . . he is such a little boy ... it infuriates me. He doesn't understanding when I tell him things . . . it's like I have to take a dictionary with me so he can translate.

Therapist: Like a parent!?

Maarja: Yes. [*Maarja laughs*]

Therapist: So do you have a sense of what might need to happen then? Do you need to let him skip into the clouds? [*referring to her ex*]

Maarja: I feel I need to let him ask if he needs some wisdom. Rather than me just giving him everything and telling him how he is.

Therapist: So it might be useful to let him live his own life.

Maarja: Of course.

Therapist: To let him go.

Maarja: Yeah.

Therapist: It doesn't mean it's easy.

Maarja: Maybe not, but he can turn to me for advice when he needs.

Therapist: And then you can live how you need to.

Maarja: Yes. Wow! [*The realisation takes Maarja by surprise*]

Therapist: Anything else you need to say?

Maarja: Thank you very much.

Therapist: It's been a wonderful learning experience. Thank you.

Session Feedback

Some months after this session, Maarja wrote and told us how much the session had impacted her life. She had quickly found the mental space to be able to make some big decisions about her relationships, and had continued to explore her life in light of what she discovered in her session. For Maarja, the most profound outcome of her past-life exploration was to be able to look at her life and herself with a new-found degree of honesty and clarity.

Idai's Past Life Session

This is another demonstration session from one of our Past Life Transpersonal Therapy workshops. Idai, as you will read below, wanted to explore the relationships between herself, her partner, and her son. She felt stuck and unable to move forward as it seemed her son was trying to control her a little too much and her partner wanted her to make a commitment she wasn't comfortable with, although she didn't know why.

You will notice that as she had experienced past life therapy before, some of the stages are not followed exactly 'by the book'. She moves naturally into the spirit realm, negotiates the confrontation and the meeting of the spirit guides with ease. She does not need to spend time describing who the character for confrontation is, nor who the spirit guides are, as she is totally immersed in the process and the dialogue is happening naturally. It's important to stay with the client's own process as they experience it.

You will also note that we don't do the 'soul – next body' dialogue. She moves beyond this stage as she immediately describes her body choice and karmic message in her process. Again, it is essential that you are flexible in your approach and go wherever the client needs to go.

Her next life seems to be this life, but she meets her parents who are giving her what she needs (that maybe they haven't yet given her in this life). It seems that they are re-parenting because of the past life resolutions she has gained.

In the processing you can see how the past life mirrors her present-day situation. For Idai, she feels a lack of freedom as she is not telling her partner how she feels, because she thinks it could kill him (metaphorically).

There is a lot to be learned and enjoyed in this fascinating session and from the feedback Idai provides at the end of the dialogue we can see the profound impact the session had on her life one year on.

Therapist: Tell me about what you would like to work on.

Idai: There's two things that are coming up, which I feel are connected. It is to do with romantic relationships, someone that I met, with whom I'm resolving karma.

So it's whether we're going to come together or we're going to go our separate ways.

But it's also to do with my son, who I feel I've had many lives with and he's been my father in many lives and that this life I'm his mother. For me, it really feels like there's a connection with these two issues. It almost feels like resolving this with my son is maybe going to open up this relationship. This is what I'm feeling.

I'm doing a lot of work on past lives. This soul keeps coming up; it's very strong. This is the recurring pattern. It's quite prominent in my life at the moment.

Therapist: What do you feel is the kind of resolution to be found? What do you feel is stuck in terms of these characters, these people in your life?

Idai: I think it's about creating harmony and balance. There appears to be blocks at the moment . . . conflict maybe because I've blamed myself previously. I've realized that it wasn't my fault so that was quite empowering because I was like, "It wasn't my fault that that happened." I think it's a recurring pattern. I just don't want to keep living every life with the same souls and having the same issues. I want to be free from it.

Therapist: It sounds like you have had enough.

Idai: Yes, and I want to free my son from it. It's almost like my father is trying to control me in the previous life and in this life, he's [*the son*] trying to control me, and he's only my six-year-old son.

Therapist: He's doing a good job.

Idai: He's doing a good job. Now I'm doing the best I can to work with it as a parent would, but there is this thing.

Therapist: Okay, all right. What's really coming to me is you've talked about here two characters, your romantic relationship and your son. Do you have any thoughts about their connection?

Idai: Yeah. It almost feels that we're meant to come together in this life.

Therapist: All three of you?

Idai: Yeah.

Therapist: Can you tell me something more about that?

Idai: You know when you go on a path and you look at the future and all that.

Therapist: Naturally.

Idai: And at the moment, only at the moment, because I feel that anything can happen. I know that the more work I do things will come together but there needs to be something that needs to happen or some resolution, some adjustments in my psyche.

Therapist: Do you make any sense of what they're meant to come together for?

Idai: Yeah, I do. I get the sense.

Therapist: You talk about almost the three of you as a unit.

Idai: Yeah, it feels like it's going to be a unit.

Therapist: And they're separate? [*questioning the status of the unit*]

Idai: It's all one.

Therapist: It's all one. Okay, all right.

Idai: But that's as it stands now.

Therapist: That's as it stands and yet what you're describing is some kind of block, some kind of conflict there.

Idai: I feel there needs to be a resolution. There is some issue that's impacting the manifestation of things progressing to where they're going to go.

Therapist: What I hear within that, what you're saying is there's some kind of impasse, there's something there that's stopping that flow and that movement of that unit's connection. Can you describe in any way, what you see is the impasse? I'm imagining almost like a brick wall. How do you experience it?

Idai: It's like . . . I would term myself an action taker. If I know what I'm shown to do next, I would do it. When I'm not shown something to do next, it's like I feel stuck. It's like okay, there's no movement. I'm not guided on what I'm going to do next. So what needs to happen? Something needs to happen inside me, is how I look at it. To me, I feel a bit stuck, I feel like my feet are stuck in the mud and so I'm looking for what needs to happen next.

Therapist: Okay. This is interesting. What I'm hearing is that what the impasse is, what the stuckness is, is you.

Idai: Yeah, it's within me.

Therapist: It's within you.

Idai: Yeah.

Therapist: It's you that is potentially stopping things from moving.

Idai: Due to my lack of awareness about something.

Therapist: Okay, is that lack of awareness stopping you from taking action?

Idai: I'm not aware of what that action is.

Therapist: Is it stopping you from taking *any* action?

Idai: Yeah.

Therapist: It's sounds like what is problematic is your lack of awareness on what the problem is for that connection to occur.

Idai: Yeah.

Therapist: I wonder what it is that is important for you to know to enable you to take the action for the connection in your life to occur, of the people and the souls – it seems that you describe as a feeling that this really should happen? How are you feeling?

Idai: Ready. It's all been a year coming.

Therapist: A whole year?

Idai: I've been working on this specific thing and for me, if I work on something [*internally*] within days, something happens, it's just very quick.

Therapist: But not this.

Idai: No.

Therapist: Not this thing. You've been working on this for a year.

Idai: Some things have been happening and having taken the necessary actions, plenty has happened. It almost feels like I'm the last hurdle if I'm honest. I don't know what's going to happen.

Therapist: All right. Let's see what happens.

Idai: If I can clear anything with these souls that needs clearing and learn the lesson that I need to learn and just see what happens, like you say, that would be great.

Therapist: It sounds like what could happen is that you might take the action that you want to take to advance this connection.

Idai: When I attract it, it will happen. It will come.

Therapist: One of the interesting things about attraction is it requires action back. You know that if you have the ability to take action, the attraction will come – the two must meet. It's never one way. It always has to be reciprocal. The action is the missing ingredient.

If we think something will happen, we can think it, think it, and then think it, and wish it and wish it and wish it. Unless we meet it by action, then it will remain where it is because it is an equal and opposite reaction. It will only move if we do. It's like you are ready for that movement to happen.

Okay. I'm feeling excited for you already.

At this stage, the hypnotic induction was induced, followed by the trance deepeners and regression bridge – back into a past life.

Therapist: Just notice where you are. Look down at your feet. What do you see there?

Idai: My feet.

Therapist: And as you look at your feet, what do you see around your feet? Where are you standing?

Idai: It's like gravelly sand.

Therapist: Gravelly and sand? Okay. I want you to just stay with your feet as you look at your feet and then move up through your ankles and into your legs. What are you noticing around your legs? Is there any clothing, or nothing at all?

Idai: I'm wearing something.

Therapist: Okay. What is it you are wearing? Describe that? What does it look like? How does it feel? What's the texture?

Idai: Something old I've had for a long time. It's just a piece of material wrapped around me.

Therapist: What colour is it?

Idai: Brown.

Therapist: All right. You're following it . . . just moving up through your body on to the top half of your body. Do you have the same piece of material or different?

Idai: It's all one.

Therapist: It's all one, okay. As you reach the top half of your body, you reach out with your hands and you look at your hands. How do they look?

Idai: I'm wearing bangles.

Therapist: You're wearing bangles. I want you to just turn your hands all the way up. You hear the bangles moving?

Idai: Yes, I hear them.

Therapist: How many are there?

Idai: Loads on each hand.

Therapist: Okay. Then I want you to reach with those hands and just hearing these bangles move, you reach up to your face and touch your cheeks. And feel the texture of your skin. How does it feel?

Idai: Smooth.

Therapist: And what kind of age does that feel?

Idai: Nineteen or twenty.

Therapist: Reach up to your hair. How does your hair feel?

Idai: Long, long straight hair.

Therapist: Are you male or female?

Idai: I'm female.

Therapist: How old do you feel?

Idai: Eighteen … nineteen.

Therapist: Female. Just eighteen, nineteen, around about that age. Then as you notice, looking around you, what do you see there?

Idai: Quite green around me.

Therapist: It's green?

Idai: Yes, it's quite green.

Therapist: And is it green grass?

Idai: Luscious.

Therapist: Luscious grass.

Idai: Luscious green and I'm sure I've got a child with me.

Therapist: How do you know?

Idai: I can see him next to me.

Therapist: You can see. Are you holding him?

Idai: He's right next to me.

Therapist: He's right next to you. On your left?

Idai: My left.

Therapist: I want you to look down at the child. Tell me what you see? Who is it?

Idai: A little boy.

Therapist: It's a little boy? What do you notice about him?

Idai: Yes. My little boy.

Therapist: Okay.

Idai: Yeah. We're together. We're one.

Therapist: What are you doing in that place?

Idai: I can see a building or something in the far distance. Maybe it's somewhere we stay or something significant and it's like a cottage or something.

Therapist: A cottage? Okay. You're there with your little boy, and you notice a cottage or something similar to that and that luscious green colour. Is it grass?

Idai: Grass. It's the trees, bushes.

Therapist: Okay. And where are you?

Idai: Feels like South India.

Therapist: Okay. You get a sense of being in that place and the essence of that. And I want you just to notice the smell there. What do you smell?

Idai: It's refreshing.

Therapist: What kind of smells is it, that refreshing smell?

Idai: Exotic. It's refreshing. It's clear. It's clean. It's pure.

Therapist: I wonder if there's anybody there around you, or if it's just you and him? It's just you two?

Idai: In this immediate space, yes.

Therapist: As you look further around you, what else do you notice?

Idai: That people are quite a distance from us and that we are in a secluded space. There's a lot of movement but not too far away, but not close by either.

Therapist: Okay.

Idai: There's a lot of hustle and bustle.

Therapist: So whereabouts are you?

Idai: We're on the edge of quite a royal or something family, living nearby, and we're just on the outskirts.

Therapist: You live there and you can see people in the distance, a hustle and a bustle. I want you just to notice what happens then?

Idai: We're just picking our food actually.

Therapist: What food are you picking?

Idai: From the trees . . . berries, and any fruits we can find. We're collecting. We take it back to the palace that we're staying in.

Therapist: Okay. Describe that palace.

Idai: It's warm in there. It's cozy. It's ours. We stay there. Me and my son live there.

Therapist: Just you two.

Idai: Just us two.

Therapist: Okay. And you get a sense of being in that place, and the smells help you, and the hustle and the bustle. What kind of time is it? What might be, and what comes to you?

Idai: 1700's. [*eighteenth century*]

Therapist: 1700's, okay. Just notice what happens next.

Idai: It seems like I go to do some work for the space that we stay in here, and I'm in and out of there quite a bit, since I'm allowed to even be staying in this place. It feels like this is a royal space.

Therapist: It's a royal space.

Idai: Feels like it's some sort of royal palace.

Therapist: You're allowed to be in there because of . . . ?

Idai: I'm allowed to be there because of the work that I'm doing.

Therapist: Because of the work that you're doing. And what kind of work is that?

Idai: What am I doing there? I do cooking, cleaning, and support. I support the [*royal*] palace it seems like.

Therapist: As you just go about your work in that place, that royal place, what happens then?

Idai: I'm going in and coming home. I'm going in and coming home.

Therapist: You just keep going about your business.

Idai: I just go about with my head down. Mostly keep my face covered up, my hair covered up. All of me covered up as a sign of respect. It's the culture. Nobody seems to notice me.

Therapist: Nobody notices you?

Idai: Not for a long time.

Therapist: What does that feel like?

Idai: I'm happy because I'm not here to cause trouble. Very quickly, people come and go when they're doing this sort of work and I know that. I'm keeping myself out of trouble, if you like.

Therapist: What kind of trouble could you get in to?

Idai: Misbehaving, stealing, and not keeping up with the duties, all those kinds of things.

Therapist: What might happen?

Idai: You'd lose your job. You'd be moved out within an instant. You could even be killed.

Therapist: Yeah. So you keep your head down?

Idai: Yeah, keeping my head down.

Therapist: You just keep busy. Do your work back and forth and back and forth.

Idai: Now, I'm noticing somebody has noticed me.

Therapist: And who might that be?

Idai: He's somebody who lives at the palace. He's a royal. A member of royalty basically.

Therapist: When you notice being noticed, what's that like?

Idai: I ignore him. I ignored him.

Therapist: And you ignored him because?

Idai: I could lose my job. I could be killed. My son could be killed.

Therapist: Because what might happen?

Idai: We'd be gone. We'd be dead. We'd be no more.

Therapist: Just by being noticed, it sounds dangerous. When you notice being noticed, what do you notice from him? He looks at you?

Idai: I don't know what he sees. I don't know. I'm covered up. I'm not making any trouble.

Why would he notice somebody like me, him being royalty? He should be after some princess out there to go near. That's why I ignore him. I don't know really what he's after. Many months go on like this.

Therapist: Okay. And it just keeps going?

Idai: He comes to visit me actually.

Therapist: Yeah. What's that like?

Idai: I sent him away. Again, I know that there are always spies and people looking around.

Therapist: That's just too dangerous.

Idai: It's just way too dangerous. We could get killed instantly here.

Therapist: Yeah?

Idai: Yep, he just keeps coming back not, giving up.

Therapist: Okay and he just keeps coming? And what happens next?

Idai: We've got to know each other a little bit now.

Therapist: All right.

Idai: We're talking a bit more.

Therapist: What's it like?

Idai: I'm still scared.

Therapist: You're still scared. You're still wary of what might happen.

Idai: Still in fear. I'm living in fear, still. I won't let anything happen.

Therapist: What's the fear that you have?

Idai: Me and my son would be killed. And he'll go happily on in his life. Nothing will change for him.

Therapist: What will you be killed for?

Idai: For playing with royalty, for messing around and it's been made clear to me what the rules are. I've seen it happen before me. I've seen others gone instantly.

Therapist: Just killed or just disappeared.

Idai: Just killed, yep.

Therapist: Because they played with royalty.

Idai: Yep. It's not the done thing.

Therapist: Then you just keep moving through time. And what happens next? What's there?

Idai: Now, my son's coming and he's going to work in there as well now. Now, it feels that we've been accepted into the space that we're working. It feels like we've been accepted at some level.

Therapist: Do you know what's happened to enable you to be accepted there?

Idai: He's had something to do with it.

Therapist: Right. He's still around then?

Idai: He's still around. He's had a lot to do with it.

Therapist: Your son is still there?

Idai: He's still there.

Therapist: This guy has made it happen in some way. And why would he have done that?

Idai: Because he knows I'm going to do things the way that's safe so that we're not killed.

Therapist: Okay.

Idai: He's been a bit smart about it.

Therapist: He's had to be smart.

Idai: And he's been strategic.

Therapist: Okay. Do you like him?

Idai: There *is* something there.

Therapist: What is that?

Idai: Something I can't explain.

Therapist: You know how that feels?

Idai: It's a knowing, yeah. It's a knowing.

Therapist: What helps you with that knowing? Do you feel it?

Idai: I know it, I feel it, and I see it. It's déjà vu. It's familiar.

Therapist: Yeah.

Idai: It's happened before.

Therapist: Okay. And I want you just to allow yourself to keep going through time and then moving forwards and then moving forwards a little more. And then what happens next?

Idai: There's a big celebration.

Therapist: Okay. What's the celebration for?

Idai: To introduce me to the whole palace as his wife.

Therapist: Okay. You're married now?

Idai: Yeah.

Therapist: And what's that like?

Idai: It's taken its time to come, so I've kind of been ready for it. I just fit in. I fit in here. I belong here. I've known everybody for years.

Therapist: Okay. Quite some time has passed?

Idai: Yeah.

Therapist: All right.

Idai: Some time. Not years.

Therapist: And this guy, he's there?

Idai: Yep. He's there holding my hand.

Therapist: How do you feel about him?

Idai: The moment here, this feels right.

Therapist: Okay. You're married now? Where's your son?

Idai: He's with me.

Therapist Okay. And you keep just moving through time, moving forwards and moving forwards and moving forwards and moving forwards, and what happens next?

Idai: It's quite difficult in here.

Therapist: Okay. Tell me about that.

Idai: I'm much protected. I've always got somebody guarding me. I was very cautious to make sure nothing happens to me. I don't have a lot of freedom. I don't have enough space of my own, or time of my own.

Therapist: What's that like?

Idai: I don't feel free here.

Therapist: And you want to feel free?

Idai: I want to feel free.

Therapist: And you don't. And where is your son?

Idai: He's off learning all the tricks in the trade, learning different trades. He's off out there learning, and comes back to me. It was quite a distance of time when he comes back. And again, he's very looked after, very guarded and very protected. He's absolutely fine.

Therapist: Good. Then you keep moving forwards through time and forwards through time and forwards through time, what happens next? [*snaps fingers*] . . . [*Idai sighs heavily.*]

Idai: As it would, being married to somebody like this, people have tried to sabotage our relationship.

Therapist: What did they try to do?

Idai: They tried to abuse me, tried to kidnap me.

Therapist: Kidnap you?

Idai: Yep.

Therapist: Wow.

Idai: Take me away from him. Make up lies. It's been really difficult. It's been really difficult actually.

Therapist: It sounds like it.

Idai: Yeah.

Therapist: How have you dealt with that? How has it been?

Idai: It's been really tough actually. It has not been joyous, happy . . . it's been a difficult marriage.

Therapist: How have you managed it?

Idai: He trusts me, actually.

Therapist: Okay.

Idai: He trusts me all but with one person.

Therapist: And who is that?

Idai: It's his best friend.

Therapist: Okay.

Idai: His best friend is not to be particularly trusted in some way, which I see, but he [*her husband*] doesn't believe me.

What happens, which I've seen before, which I know, is he's intoxicated me, abused me.

Therapist: The guy? Your husband?

Idai: His best friend.

Therapist: His best friend, okay.

Idai: Behind the other one's back. My husband's found out and he died instantly of a heart attack.

Therapist: Your husband died?

Idai: Yeah, because he has found out everything that's happened.

Therapist: He was shocked? Because he's found out what the other guy's done, his friend, to you? And how is this for you?

Idai: I go into a deep darkness. I don't come in that life; just wear white . . . I've no interest in the world.

Therapist: It's just . . . everything in a way . . . ends?

Idai: Shriveled.

Therapist: Shriveled.

Idai: Just no life.

Therapist: Okay. How is that?

Idai: I don't like it.

Therapist: You don't like it?

Idai: No. It's a waste of life and I'm still young.

Therapist: How young?

Idai: By now, I've been in my twenties somewhere, late twenties.

Therapist: Yeah. And life has almost just finished. Okay. I want you just to keep moving forwards through time now. I want you to keep moving forwards a little faster, a little faster. I want you to go right towards the end of your life, right towards the end of your life and just getting right towards the end of your life. I want you to notice where you are and what's happening there. Where are you?

Idai: I'm kind of shut away.

Therapist: Where?

Idai: I'm ignored. It's like I'm in the prison quarters or something.

Therapist: What's your age?

Idai: I feel like I'm about . . . coming up to sixty.

Therapist: Sixty? It's been a long time.

Idai: Yeah.

Therapist: And you're shut away?

Idai: Yep. They shut me away.

Therapist: Okay. I want you to notice the thoughts that you have about your life and how you feel about it. Tell me what is that like?

Idai: Don't ever marry into royalty! [*she laughs*]

Therapist: Don't marry into royalty!

Idai: Yeah. Because otherwise, you just don't live happily.

Therapist: Yeah.

Idai: It's not going to make you happy.

Therapist: All right.

Idai: Your people will die. You'll lose your loved ones and you'll be shut away, put way, and ignored.

Therapist: I want you just to notice coming towards the end of your life. This is going to be the final moment when you take your final breath. I'm going to count to ten back to one and when we reach one, it's the end.

Ten, just taking your final breaths, nine, eight and seven and six and five and four and three, and two, and one [*snaps fingers*] and just find yourself floating . . . just floating in between. As you float in between, you find yourself there in that magical place of in between lives. There you're able to come in to contact with the person that you found it so hard to talk to.

I want you to notice who it is there that you're able to speak to, that you were never able to say those things that you needed to say in that previous life. Just have them there in front of you and tell me what you have. Who is that?

Idai: He's there.

Therapist: Which he is he?

Idai: My husband in the previous life. He's there.

Therapist: Okay, alright. Now there, what are you able to say to him that you weren't able to say before?

Idai: **So** now, my son . . . I feel his presence by me, just his energy with me.

Therapist: Okay.

Idai: But I've said to him we need to move away, we cannot live here.

Therapist: You've said to your husband that you need to move away, that you can't be in that place.

Idai: We can't live together in this palace happily.

Therapist: And what does he say to you?

Idai: We're talking about it for some time actually.

Therapist: How does this discussion go?

Idai: He's open to listening.

Therapist: Okay.

Idai: We share our views openly.

Therapist: And what are your views? You said, "We can't live here. We can't live in this palace." And what are his views?

Idai: I told him it's dangerous and eventually he agrees. He agrees. He agrees we cannot live happily the way we need to and want to in this place.

Therapist: Okay.

Idai: He comes around.

Therapist: All right.

Idai: And then actually he's just taking over and he's ready to make things happen.

Therapist: He's ready to change things?

Idai: Yes, we're going to.

Therapist: You're going to work together and go somewhere else together? What's changed for him with what you've said?

Idai: He won't die of a heart attack. He won't die of a heart attack, from a broken heart.

Therapist: Okay. And where is your son?

Idai: He stays with me. His presence is always with me.

Therapist: His presence is with you?

Idai: Yeah.

Therapist: Is there anything else you need to say to your husband that you couldn't say before? Or is that enough?

Idai: He agrees that it's time for a clean break. He needs it actually.

Therapist: What is the clean break for him?

Idai: Get away from everybody.

Therapist: Like who?

Idai: His family, his friends. And actually he needs to leave some people behind. People had been holding him back, taking him down different paths. He's beginning to see more differently.

Therapist: I want you to begin to just become aware of that shift and that movement, and that change and that connection, and just drifting with him to wherever that place is that the two of you connect. What's that like? How does it feel?

Idai: There's movement and it's quite expansive. It's freedom.

Therapist: Freedom.

Idai: Yeah.

Therapist: Okay. As you experience that freedom, just enable the freedom to keep moving with you now beginning to move in that place through eternity within you. As that begins to move with you for the rest of time, appearing from within that and emerging from within that are your spirit guides.

They're enabling you the wisdom that you really can hear and feel and sense. What is it they are able to offer you? What guidance can you experience from them? What is the gift in this place for you, readying you for the next time, the next place, and the next life?

Idai: This time it will be fine. This time it will be different.

Therapist: Did they tell you how?

Idai: Just keep taking the steps.

Therapist: Keep taking the steps.

Idai: As I'm guided to.

Therapist: As they're guiding you to, keep taking the steps.

Idai: They're showing me every step of the way. I don't need to be worried about anything. There's nothing to be scared of. They are with me every single step of the way.

Therapist: Guiding you?

Idai: I feel that. I feel it now.

Therapist: You feel that? Where do you feel it?

Idai: It's the calmness and stillness I have when I take action.

Therapist: That's the calmness and the stillness from them guiding you. They're with you. You can feel it now. Okay.

I want you to become aware of whereabouts you feel it around you. Is it from behind, the side, or in front? Where is it?

Idai: All over. It's like I'm cocooned in it.

Therapist: Okay.

Idai: I feel it in my breath while I'm breathing.

Therapist: It feels like breathing differently. They're guiding you, letting you know that they're with you every step of the way, they're there. With each action that you take, they're guiding you.

And emerging from within that, I want you to begin to become aware of an essence, just an essence within you there, within that place, an essence of the next life to come. And presenting itself out of that next life to come is the body that you're going to be situating yourself in. There's a selection of them for you to choose. These bodies will be situated in certain places with certain people. And you're able to choose the body that you're going to take into the next life. Tell me which one it is? What is it about that?

Idai: Like environments and families and . . .

Therapist: Yeah. [*she laughs*]

Idai: Okay. What is it about that? I'm thinking what have I let myself in for.

Therapist: Okay. What have you let yourself in for? What body have you chosen?

Idai: Where I will be challenged the most.

Therapist: Where you'll be challenged the most. And tell me more about that.

Idai: Where I'll evolve the most on a soul level. That's what I've picked.

Therapist: Alright. Describe it to me.

Idai: It's not that it's terrible. It's just I do experience a lot of difficulties in all areas of my life, and learn lessons it seems in all areas of my life, and to learn from it and evolve from it, and then also to show others the way. But I also have the freedom as well which is quite interesting. I've chosen the body where I will have the freedom to evolve culturally within my environment, my parents.

Therapist: Okay.

Idai: It's the right one.

Therapist: It's a knowing.

Idai: Yeah.

Therapist: Okay. I want you just to become aware of that knowing to allow yourself to get closer, move closer into that body, that choice and beginning to get closer and moving into that body, ten, getting closer, nine and eight and seven, six and five and four, getting closer and closer, soon becoming, and three and two and one, [*snaps fingers*] in that body. I want you just to be in that body, in that place, cocooned. I want you to notice where the light is. Where is it?

Idai: It's all around me.

Therapist: It's all around you. I want you to just pinpoint that light down into one specific place. Locate it and start to move towards it. You're getting closer and closer, and getting closer and closer. And ten, getting closer and closer now, nine and eight, and seven, and six, getting closer and closer to the next life. The next life that you emerge into, and five, and four, and three, nearly there, nearly there, nearly all the way back through into that life, and two and one. There I want you to look down at your feet and tell me what you notice.

Idai: The ground, my shoes.

Therapist: And you recognise those shoes? And look up your legs and what do you notice there?

Idai: Familiar.

Therapist: It's familiar. What's familiar?

Idai: It's what I've chosen.

Therapist: It's what you've chosen.

Idai: What I've chosen.

Therapist: Okay. And you look up at your body, and at your hands. You feel your face. Where are you?

Idai: I chose to be here.

Therapist: And what age is it? What era is it? What is the number of the year?

Idai: Nineteen something.

Therapist: Nineteen something. Okay. I just want you to notice where you are and who you're with.

Idai: It's this lifetime.

Therapist: This lifetime. Okay I want you just to be aware of being of this lifetime. I want you just to notice how you feel here in this lifetime.

Idai has gone into her current lifetime, hence there is no need to further establish what past life she is in.

Idai: I can see my mum, my dad, my siblings, and where I live. Yep, I'm familiar with all of this.

Therapist: Okay. It's this lifetime, all right. I want you just to be aware of all of that around you. I want you just to notice what you've brought into this lifetime from that experience of that previous life and the 'in between' and all that happened there. What do you notice?

Idai: Very strongly my mum and dad, and what a fantastic job they do making this all happen for me. I'm actually amazed. I actually feel really amazed.

Therapist: What's amazing you like that?

Idai: Of the good job they've done. [*Idai laughs, with a tone of surprise*]

Therapist: What amazes you about it?

Idai: That I learned everything I needed to learn. I'm learning everything I need to learn by choosing them as my parents, and what a gift they have been. I'm absolutely amazed.

Therapist: Okay.

Idai: We're standing strong together. I'm looking at them.

Therapist: All right.

Idai: And actually, there's a communication going on.

Therapist: Tell me about that.

Idai: They are actually really proud of me, which they've never said to me before.

Therapist: But they're telling you?

Idai: They're telling me here. They've never told me in the physical world.

Therapist: What are they saying?

Idai: They're clapping their hands. They're jumping up and down [*At this stage Idai starts to laugh with disbelief*]. They're really proud of me, and that they're sorry they've never been able to tell me in real life and they wouldn't change a thing about me.

And that I've had a huge impact on their lives. That I've helped them to grow more than I'll never know. I never got this from my mum and dad. But that was a gift. That was all part of them, all part of the journey.

Therapist: And now you have it because of what's changed?

Idai: I never experienced this with my mum and dad together.

Therapist: How does it feel?

Idai: It's like a relief . . . that this is all meant to be like this. I actually feel more of an acceptance of my body that I chose, the challenges that I've chosen, the lessons I've chosen to learn. They're actually waving me goodbye now. They've told me that I'm ready to go.

Therapist: Okay.

Idai: I'm ready to leave the nest, it's my time.

Therapist: It's your time.

Idai: Now, I've got this huge [*she laughs again*] . . . I've got all my friends and family behind them now, all waving me goodbye.

Therapist: You're ready.

Idai: And it's all happening around the house, the street where we live. It seems quite significant. They're waving me goodbye now and I'm happy, they're all happy.

Therapist: Okay. What's it like?

Idai: My son's back with me. He's actually on my right hand now. I don't know what the significance is.

Therapist: What's it like for you him being on the right side as opposed to the left side?

Idai: Very interesting.

Therapist: What's interesting?

Idai: Because he's always on my left. It's like I feel stronger.

Therapist: You feel stronger with him?

Idai: Yeah, today now. I feel like it's time to go.

Therapist: Okay. To go where?

Idai: Wherever I need to go next. Start a new life, who knows, go anywhere, go abroad, anything.

Therapist: Yeah.

Idai: Anything's possible it seems like. It feels like when I got married before, it felt very different. It feels like me leaving now, it's very different.

Therapist: What's different about it?

Idai: It's more joyous for some reason. Yeah, it's just completely different energy.

Therapist: Yeah. I want you just to keep that within you, notice where you keep the energy. And there's more?

Idai: There's a guy behind us now and he's taking us with him.

Therapist: What guy is this?

Idai: The one that I've met in the previous life in between lives.

Therapist: Right. What's he doing?

Idai: He's taking us.

Therapist: He's taking you? And how is that?

Idai: And everyone's waving us goodbye and it's all happy and what is it like? It's just effortless.

Therapist: Okay. It sounds like it's meant to be.

Idai: We move away. That's the difference this time.

Therapist: It's important that you move away, that those ties are broken. But it sounds like there's a blessing there, that it's okay for that to happen, from different places, from different people. And you're able to go now. Okay, that's good.

Then I want you just to take a deep breath in. Just take a deep breath in. I want you just to become aware of whatever time that is, that place, those people, where you're heading, and how you feel.

Notice the position of your son on your right side. Notice being able to leave with those blessings, with that freedom that you so desire, feeling free, drifting into the freedom and through time whatever time you're in, moving up, moving forwards as much as you need to bring you back into this place and this time. Drifting back into this place and this time, right the way back up, ten, moving back up, nine and eight and seven, and six, moving right the way back up through time. And five and four, and three and two nearly all the way back to this time and this place, and one [*snaps fingers*]. Here sitting on the chair, your hands resting, your feet on the floor, feeling your heartbeat and your breathing, free and ready.

Now we move into the 'processing' part of the session and explore what the experience was like for Idai and what she has discovered.

Idai: Wow. Was that real? Was that real?

Therapist: How was it?

Idai: Surprising.

Therapist: What a journey. Tell me about the surprise. What's the surprise?

Idai: It feels right why I'm resisting any movement.

Therapist: What connection have you made?

Idai: In that life, I killed somebody. Well, not due to my . . . because we stayed in the palace. It led to his death. That is what I'm avoiding for whatever reason unconsciously.

Therapist: Now.

Idai: Yeah. Because of his ideals, how he wants life to be.

Therapist: Which is?

Idai: Which is somebody who's going to be moving with him and . . .

Therapist: Into his palace.

Idai: Yeah, into his palace [*she laughs as we together recognise she is talking about her current partner*].

Therapist: Wow, it's his palace.

Idai: Yeah, into his life.

Therapist: Symbolically.

Idai: Symbolically.

Therapist: Yeah, royalty?

Idai: No . . . but that's how I envisioned it, how I'm avoiding that happening.

Therapist: So is it this situation that he wants to move into his house and everything sort of stays there, as it is, and . . . what then for you?

Idai: It feels like I want to have freedom. I'd be trapped.

Therapist: Okay. As happened previously. And now, what needs to happen?

Idai: We need to move away. We need to move away.

Therapist: Well, is there a conversation that needs to happen first?

Idai: Yeah, exactly. There is a conversation.

Therapist: And how do you envision this conversation going?

Idai: Gosh. I can't tell him all this stuff, can I?

Therapist: Well, you could tell him about the reason why you need to leave, but maybe this is not the best way to put it across.

Idai: No.

Therapist: The conversation that you need to have is something more about . . . you *need* to retain your sense of freedom. How do you imagine if you have the conversation for example, how do you imagine the conversation would go? How would he receive this kind of a need from you because it's a need, right? It's important, it's a lesson that you've now revisited and become aware of, and worked with, and now it has to be. How's he going to take it?

Idai: He's going to take time to consider it.

Therapist: Okay.

Idai: He's not going to instantly say no. He will know, knowing me there's a good reason for it or else it's not going to kill him. I'm not going to say that's going to happen but he'll know after some thought that there'll be reason why I said it. And he'll take it seriously.

Therapist: You feel confident of that?

Idai: There's certain stages that need to happen before this conversation will happen. Let's put it that way.

Therapist: And do you know what those stages are? You get the sense of what needs to occur?

Idai: Yes.

Therapist: You know?

Idai: Yeah, I know.

Therapist: Alright. Good. Tell me . . . your son . . . how does he fit into this?

Idai: I was looking for him to communicate with me with anything he had to tell me . . . but I wasn't picking anything up. He seemed quite content with me, which surprised me. And actually that's why he's chosen to be with me in this life because actually he seeks the freedom as well and the space just like me.

Therapist: Yeah. And the guy, why do you get a sense he's chosen you also?

Idai: In this life?

Therapist: Yeah, your guy.

Idai: I don't know. Why do I get that sense? Why has he chosen me?

Therapist: Has he told you?

Idai: He can't tell me yet, can't tell me yet.

Therapist: Do you need to know?

Idai: I would need to know, wouldn't I? I think it's got to be a two-way thing. Expression of emotion, there's a block from his path. That is the thing that needs to happen next.

Therapist: All right. So this sounds like one of the steps that needs to happen before the conversation.

Idai: That's what I'm saying, that it needs to happen before that.

Therapist: Okay. Is it going too far for me to say that therefore what you describe at the beginning of this session about this impasse is not entirely all yours, am I right?

Idai: Yeah.

Therapist: Something needs to meet, that needs to be that joining, a reciprocal togetherness.

Idai: I can only do my part and be responsible for my part.

Therapist: Are you good enough?

Idai: Yeah.

Therapist: Okay, good. Wow. Thank you very much.

Idai: Thank you.

SESSION FEEDBACK

About a year after this session, Idai kindly shared with us the impact of her Past Life Transpersonal Therapy experience. These are her words.

> "Since the session last year, I could write a book as to what life has revealed to me in one year alone. I have stayed

committed and continued to dig into my past and clear, release and re-write my future as much as I can.

The story of my life has continued to include significant healing and clearing of past life repercussions in all areas of my life. Based on what I experienced one year ago, life has upgraded me in all areas – significantly.

After endless years of clearing and removing blocks, externally I am beginning to see the fruits of all this intense growth and shedding of lifetimes of pain and trauma. I am taking massive and bold actions and walking paths I once never could have dreamed I would be taking. Life has become much more effortless in so many ways, and yet I am aware there is always more to uncover and release.

The session hugely impacted my whole life as after that day, I made big new decisions about myself and my life. From then on the ripple effects are what I am living now. The session was a highlight in my life so far in terms of personal development at the highest, truest, most genuine and on a spiritual and soul level.

The session brought great peace into my life and I will always be grateful for it. It felt like life had lined me up to be there to take part in that transformative experience. Thanks to you both, Tom and Sandra, for creating such a powerful process."

This session shows how remarkable Past Life Transpersonal Therapy is for clearing blocks, fostering growth, and healing long-held pain. Idai experienced life-changing effects that impacted her on multiple levels.

We move now to our final chapter of this book, and our parting thoughts.

Chapter 12
Parting Thoughts

Reading furnishes the mind only with materials of knowledge;
it is thinking that makes what we read ours.
John Locke

We are now at the end of this journey. We hope you have enjoyed this book and that our words have opened you to more of yourself. As ever when writing a book, the end product has become so much more than we envisaged when we started. This project has grown, as we have done, through exploring and evolving our thoughts.

Healing from the Other Side attempts to unite a multitude of theoretical concepts from psychology, psychotherapy, philosophy, spirituality, and past life therapy – from both eastern and western traditions. Our aim in this work is to bring alignment to the brain, mind, body, and soul for a deeper connection with ourselves. Bringing together the ideas that have shaped our work with past life therapy over the years has certainly got us thinking deeper of the infinite possibilities of discovery when stepping beyond the present day, into the realms of the immortal soul, moving from body-to-body, from life-to-life.

Our intention has been for you to see how essential imagination and creativity are in connecting our mind, brain, body, and soul for the process of healing and resolving issues. Past Life Transpersonal Therapy is one of the most creative forms of therapy you can engage in. We have both personally benefitted from past life therapy and have been deeply moved and changed by it, as have the people in the case studies presented in this book, and the many people we have worked with both individually and on our courses.

Even if you still don't believe in the notion of past lives, or that past life therapy can accurately uncover your past lives, this approach undeniably heals and connects you deeper within yourself – and therein lies its unquestionable power.

Scientific proof, whilst understandably attractive, becomes obsolete when you read and hear first-hand about the profound changes people have made in themselves and their lives having experienced this process. It most definitely resolves numerous physical and psychological symptoms. But what makes it so transformative?

Is it because you are re-experiencing an original trauma (from whatever life) and releasing the emotional charge? Is it from the comfort that is gained from discovering that your soul never dies, or understanding the karmic imprint and message that has led to your current life symptoms? Could it be because you have connected with your hidden strengths or found your direction and purpose in your life, leaving you with a new sense of meaning, creativity, empowerment, and inner peace? Maybe some or all of these have made the difference. As Brian Weiss says, past life therapy gives individuals "new handles and hooks for approaching and grasping their experiences" (1995, p. 104). Whatever the reason for the transformation, Past Life Transpersonal Therapy facilitates a deep healing that is undeniable.

We hope you have gained some clarity from our time together. Maybe it is time now to pass this book to somebody else. Give someone you know who may be seeking some answers to questions they have about life the gift of discovering *their* eternal being. Whoever this might be, you'll pass it onto them for a very good reason. And at some point, in one of your future lives when you meet them again, you might well discover what that reason was.

For now, if our paths don't cross in this life . . . we'll look forward to meeting you in another one, whenever and wherever that may be!

'Kindred hearts no distance parts.'
~ *James Lendall Basford* ~

APPENDIX

THE PAST LIFE TRANSPERSONAL THERAPY™ PROCESS

1. **The step-by-step hypnotic induction specific to Past Life Transpersonal Therapy.**

I. Settling down and connecting.
II. Physical bodily relaxation.
III. Mind relaxation.
IV. Deepening process.
V. Regressing the experience back in this life and into the womb, then following the light back into the past life.

2. **Embodiment of the past life character: keeping in the 'past-present' tense and in the past life body.**

- As you look down at your feet, what are you wearing?
- Looking up at your legs, what do you have on?
- Beginning to describe your upper body – what are you wearing?
- Notice looking around you, and what are you seeing?
- Are you alone or with others?
- How old do you feel there? (Not how old *are* you? This can alert logic.)
- What is the year? (If they are young they may not know this.)

3. **Establishing the scene in detail: E.g., Where are you? Who else is there? What do you see? What else?**

- What is that like?
- Where are you there?
- When is that? What is the year?

- What is it that you're doing there?
- How are you feeling about what you are doing?
- What's really important for you right now?
- What's troubling you?
- How do you feel about your life?

4. Exploring the past life. How the life is lived and develops.

- Move them forwards in age from each past life scene.

"In a moment I am going to count to three and snap my fingers and you will have transported to a few hours forwards in time there . . . one, two, three [snap] *. . . what's happening there?"*

- Where are you in your life there? What is it like?
- How are you feeling?
- What's really important for you there?
- What is concerning for you?
- What would you like to do in your future?
- What do you dream of?

5. Moving to the moment of death and discovery of what's learnt from the moment of death, through to the death transition.

"In a moment I am going to count to three and snap my fingers and you will have transported to the last day of your life . . . one, two, three [snap] *. . . what's happening there?"*

After the scene has been explored, you need to move to the time of death.

"And then in a moment I am going to count to three and snap my fingers and you will have transported to a time just before you take your last breath, one, two, three [snap]*."*

- What's happening there? Who is around you?
- What thoughts do you die with?
- What feelings do you leave that life with?
- What meaning do you become aware of from the nature of your death?

Then . . . *"And as you pass over, you find that you are floating up out of your body, looking down at the scene before you . . ."*

- Is there anything that you notice now that you have left your body form?

6. **Transcending to the spirit realm, to uncover all the messages that can be gathered.**

Then . . . *"And as you continue to float up away from that scene and into the sky . . . travelling up . . . floating . . . seeing the ground getting further and further away . . . into a place where you can see the world below you . . ."*

". . . then in a moment I am going to count to three and snap my fingers and you will have transported yourself into the spirit realm . . . one, two, three [snap]."

7. **Confrontation.**

In the confrontation phase within the spirit realm, the meeting of the 'conflict' person or persons in the previous life takes place.

"In a moment you are going to speak with the person from your past life that you most need to resolve something with, and that you can now confront with what you need to say. As I count to three and snap my fingers, that person appears . . . one, two, three [snap]."

You then begin to guide your client to consider the following questions and then formulate what they would like to say to that person.

- What happened and how has it impacted you?
- How do you feel about what happened?
- What do you think about what happened?
- What is left with you?

Guide them then to tell the 'problem' person what they need to say. The 'conflict' person responds, to share their experience of the situation. Continue the dialogue between them until you feel everything has been expressed and some new insights and resolution has been gained.

8. Meeting the spirit guides.

"And then in a moment I am going to count to three and snap my fingers and your spirit guides will come forward to you . . . one, two, three [snap] *. . . Your spirit guide is the one who indeed has all the wisdom and knowledge about you and your life and holds all you need to know for your future lives. It is time now for you to greet your spirit guide and invite them to speak or convey a message to you in any way that is appropriate . . . all you need to do is listen and hear – listen and hear – and allow yourself to be open to the message your spirit guide is offering you."*

Once the message has been listened to and shared with you (the therapist) . . .

"And is there anything you need to ask to fully understand and accept this message?"

9. The next life body choice process – choosing the next body form.

"And then in a moment I am going to count to three and snap my fingers and you will see ahead of you a selection of body forms for you to choose your next body for your next life . . . one, two, three [snap]*."*

- How many body choices do you have?

"And in a moment, you can try some of these possible choices on . . . So, as you choose the first body to try on . . ."

- How does it fit?
- What does it feel like?
- How does it move?
- What does each body offer?
- What do you notice about that body?
- What might be your mission in this body?
- Which body do you choose?

When each body has been tried on (to a maximum of three), then move them into the body choice for the next life.

"And as you have tried those bodies on, now move to the body choice for your next life . . ."

10. Dialoguing with the future self.

"In a moment you are going to speak with your future self, your soon-to-be-born incarnation – your body and self to be . . . Begin now to reach out and touch the chosen body of your future self. Hold your body's face or hand tenderly, feel your future body's skin, look into their eyes, and smell their scent. Begin then to tell your future self what it needs to hear right now . . ."

Guide your client to tell their future self what will most help them live a life of alignment, in accordance with the message and spirit of karma, as well as what will best enable them to live life in harmony with their purpose and life mission.

Then, suggest that they become quiet, and . . . listen . . .

After a short time, suggest imagining becoming their future 'self to be', who has just heard this message.

"And then in a moment I am going to count to three and snap my fingers and then you will become your future self . . . one, two, three [snap]."

- And then ask the following questions, giving some time for responses:

"And as your future self . . ."

- What would you like to say back in response to what you've heard?
- How do you feel about the learnings that have been conveyed to you?
- What do you make of 'who' you are?
- How does it feel to know the purpose of your being?

"And then in a moment I am going to count to three and snap my fingers and then you will return to the spirit realm . . . one, two, three [snap] . . ."

- And having heard that, what might you want to say back?

Continue swapping back and forth for a period of time to enable to dialogue to elicit what needs to be made explicit. Then it will be time to proceed to the next life.

11. Integration into the next or current life.

Having chosen the next body to be and engaged in the dialogue that passes over the karmic message and learning from the spirit realm, it is then time to begin entering the next life, which could be the client's current life. From the spirit realm, we then re-enact the regression visualisation of looking for the light, only this time, the light leads to the next incarnation, into the womb of the mother of their future life, into the being they have just dialogued with.

Once you have guided the rebirth and they have arrived in the next life, you then begin to explore that incarnation as before, starting at step 2 of the Past Life Transpersonal Therapy process.

12. Returning to the present and the learning exploration.

After a maximum of two past lives it will become appropriate to return to the current life experience.

You ask them to choose their present body form, and then find the light back into the birth of their current life growing back up to their current age. Once the chronological age has been reached, you instruct the client to open their eyes and begin the final phase of processing the experience.

Use both open and closed questions to help them verbalise their experience. The focus is on exploring what has been learned, what the meaning is in this life, and what has been healed through this experience. How what that? What did you notice that resonated with your current life? What surprised you? What have your learned?

Resources

To further support you in your journey with Past Life Transpersonal Therapy™, you can obtain a further twenty sessions of video instruction to bring this book to life, which are optimised for PC/Mac and all mobile formats such as tablets and phones. Included are over two hours of live demonstrations, presentation slides, and audio downloads. To access all of these learning materials see:

- **www.HealingFromTheOtherSide.com**

For more information on the use and application of hypnosis see:

- **www.HypnosisResourceHub.com**

To find out how you can train on one of our worldwide Past Life Transpersonal Therapy™ practitioner programmes see:

- **www.PLTT.co.uk**

To find out about other training programmes run by Dr Tom Barber and Dr Sandra Westland, visit Contemporary College of Therapeutic Studies.

- **www.ContemporaryCollege.com**

For personal development and self-help resources developed by Dr Tom Barber and Dr Sandra Westland see:

- **www.SelfHelpSchool.com**

To visit Tom and Sandra's personal therapy websites see:

- **www.DrTomBarber.com**
- **www.DrSandraWestland.com**

BIBLIOGRAPHY

Augustine, R., & Pine-Coffin, S. (Trans.). (1970). *Confessions*. New York: Penguin Group.

Avraam-Repa, M. (2013). Regression Therapy and Past Lives: A Critical Approach. Interview with Dr V. Rodrigues. *Phenomena, 152*, 18–23.

Baker, M. C., & Goetz, S. (2011). *The Soul Hypothesis*. London: Continuum Books.

Barber, T., & Westland, S. (2010). *Thinking Therapeutically: Hypnotic Skills and Strategies Explored.* Carmarthen: Crown House Publishing.

Battino, R., & South, T. (2005). *Ericksonian Approaches: A Comprehensive Manual*. Carmarthen: Crown House Publishing.

Botkin, A., & Hogan, C. (2005). *Induced After Death Communication*. Charlottesville: Hampton Roads Publishing.

Bowman, C. (1998). *Children's Past Lives: How Past Life Memories Affect Your Child*. New York: Bantam Books.

Brun, B., Pederson, E., & Runberg, M. (1993). *Symbols of the Soul: Therapy and Guidance through Fairy Tales*. London: Jessica Kingsley.

Buonomano, D. (2017). *Your Brain is a Time Machine: The Neuroscience and Physics of Time.* New York: W. W. Norton & Company.

Byrne, R. (2006). *The Secret*. London: Simon & Schuster.

Callaway, E. (1975). Brain Potentials and Prediction of Performance. In N. Burch & H. Altshuler (Eds.), *Behavior and Brain Electrical Activity (pp. 473-480)*. New York: Plenum Press.

Chinen, A. B. (1996). The Emergence of Transpersonal Psychiatry. In B.W. Scotton, A.B. Chinen, & J. R. Battista, (Eds.), *Textbook of Transpersonal Psychiatry and Psychology (pp. 9-18)*. New York: Basic Books.

Collins, R. (2011). A Scientific Case for the Soul. In M. Baker, & S. Goetz, *The Soul Hypothesis: Investigations into the Existence of the Soul (pp. 222-246)*. New York: Continuum.

Consciousness. In *Merriam-Webster Dictionary*. Retrieved from https://www.merriam-webster.com/dictionary/consciousness

Cooper, L., & Erickson, M. H. (2002). *Time Distortion in Hypnosis* (2nd ed.). Carmarthen: Crown House Publishing.

Csikszentmihalyi, M. (2004, February). *Flow, the Secret to Happiness* [Video file]. Retrieved from https://www.ted.com/talks/mihaly_csikszentmihalyi_on_flow

Damasio, A. (2000). *The Feeling of What Happens: Body, Emotion and the Making of Consciousness*. London: Vintage.

Donne, J. (1988). *No Man is an Island*. London: Souvenir Press.

Edelstein, B. (2011, April 08). *Bringing Awe into the Equation: Exploring Personal Stories of Profound Transformation* [Blog post]. Retrieved from https://www.psychologytoday.com/blog/authentic-engagement/201104/bringing-awe-the-equation

Erickson, M. H. (1991). *My Voice Will Go with You: Teaching Tales of Milton H. Erickson*. New York: W. W. Norton & Company.

Fallio, V. (2007). *New Developments in Consciousness Research*. New York: Nova Science Publishers, Inc.

Fechner, G. T. (1904). *The Little Book of Life after Death*. Boston: Little, Brown and Company.

Fell, J., Axmacher, N., & Haupt, S. (2010). From alpha to gamma: Electrophysiological correlates of meditation-related states of consciousness. *Medical Hypotheses*, *75*(2), 218-224.

Feuerstein, M. (2013). *Health Psychology: A Psychobiological Perspective*. New York: Springer.

Friedman, H. L., & Hartelius, G. (Eds.). (2015). *The Wiley-Blackwell Handbook of Transpersonal Psychology.* West Sussex: Wiley-Blackwell.

Gentile, L., Cebrià, F., & Bartscherer, K. (2011). The Planarian Flatworm: An in Vivo Model for Stem Cell Biology and Nervous System Regeneration. *Disease Models and Mechanisms*, *4*, 12–19.

Gracian, B., & Jacobs, J. (Trans.) (2017). *The Art of Worldly Wisdom.* Los Angeles: Enhanced Media Publishing.

Grof, C., & Grof, S. (1990). *The Stormy Search for the Self: A Guide to Personal Growth through Transformational Crises*. Los Angeles: Jeremey P. Tarcher.

Grof, S., & Grof, C. (2010). *Holotropic Breathwork: A New Approach to Self-Exploration and Therapy.* New York: Excelsior Editions.

Grof, S. (1979). *Realms of the Human Unconscious*. London: Souvenir Press.

Hadalski, K. R. (2011). *Karma: How to View it, Use it, and Lose it*. Salt Lake City: Millennial Mind Publishing.

Hammond, C. (2013). *Time Warped: Unlocking the Mysteries of Time Perception*. Edinburgh: Canongate Books.

Harrold, G. (2011). *The Answer: Supercharge the Law of Attraction and Find the Secret to True Happiness*. London: Orion.

Hay, L. (1984). *You Can Heal Your Life*. London: Hay House.

Heidegger, M. (1927/1962). *Being and Time*. New York: Harper & Row.

Henry, R. C. (2005). The Mental Universe. *Nature, 436*(7047), 29.

Howe, L. (2009). *How to Read the Akashic Records: Accessing the Archive of the Soul and its Journey*. Boulder: Sounds True, Inc.

Humphreys, C. (1995). *Karma and Rebirth: The Karmic Law of Cause and Effect*. London: Routledge.

Hunter, C. R. (2010). *The Art of Hypnosis: Mastering Basic Techniques*. Carmarthen: Crown House Publ ishing.

Hunter, C. R. (2016). *The Art of Spiritual Hypnosis: Accessing Divine Wisdom*. New York: Blooming Twig Books.

Hunter, C. R., & Eimer, B. N. (2012). *The Art of Hypnotic Regression Therapy*. Carmarthen: Crown House Publishing.

James, T., & Woodsmall, W. (1989). *Time Line Therapy and the Basis of Personality*. Carmarthen: Crown House Publishing.

Jirsch, A., & Courtenay, A. (2013). *Create Your Perfect Future.* London: Piatkus Books.

Jirsch, A., & Cafferky, M. (2011). *The Future is Yours: Introducing Future Life Progression*. London: Piatkus Books.

Jones, D. E. (2000). *An Instinct for Dragons*. New York: Routledge.

Jung, C. G. (1968). *Archetypes and the Collective Unconscious*. New York: Princeton University Press.

Jung, C. G. (1976). *Psychological Types: The Collected Works of C. G. Jung*, Vol. 6 (Bollingen Series XX). Princeton: Princeton University Press.

Jung, C. G. (2004). *Four Archetypes*. London: Routledge.

Kant, I., & Smith, N. K. (1929). *Immanuel Kant's Critique of Pure Reason*. Boston: Bedford.

Kasprow, C., & Scotton, B. (1999). A Review of Transpersonal Theory and its Application to the Practice of Psychotherapy. *The Journal of Psychotherapy Practice and Research, 8*(1), 12–23.

Koloski, B. E. (2017). *Your Journey Was Never Meant to End: A Compelling Case for Reincarnation*. Portland: PublishNation.

Kyabgon, T. (2015). *Karma: What It Is, What It Isn't, Why It Matters*. Boston: Shambhala Publications.

Lajoie, D. H., & Shapiro, S. I. (1992). Definitions of Transpersonal Psychology: The First Twenty-Three Years. *Journal of Transpersonal Psychology, 24*(1), 74-98.

Lucas, S. (2008). *Past Life Dreamwork: Healing the Soul through Understanding Karmic Patterns*. Vermont: Bear & Company.

Lovejoy, G. (2017). *Revolutionize Your Self: Transcend Your Ego False Self, Embrace Your Authentic True Self*. Bloomington: Balboa Press.

Matousek, M. (2017). *Writing to Awaken: A Journey of Truth, Transformation, and Self-Discovery*. California: New Harbinger.

May, R. (1972). *Power and Innocence: A Search for the Sources of Violence*. New York: W. W. Norton & Company, Inc.

May, R. (2012/1950). *The Meaning of Anxiety*. New York: W. W. Norton & Company. Kindle file.

Merleau-Ponty, M. (1945/2002). *Phenomenology of Perception*. London: Routledge.

Miller, D. L. (1981). *The New Polytheism: Rebirth of the Gods and Goddesses*. Dallas: Spring Publications.

Minkowski, E. (1970). *Lived Time: Phenomenological and Psychopathological Studies,* (Northwestern University Studies in Phenomenology & Existential Philosophy). Illinois: Northwestern University Press.

Newton, M. (2004). *Life Between Lives: Hypnotherapy for Spiritual Regression*. Minnesota: Llewellyn Publications.

Pennebaker, J. (2004). *Writing to Heal: A Guided Journal for Recovering from Trauma and Emotional Upheaval*. California: New Harbinger.

Raffensperger, C. (2012, April). *Becoming Great Ancestors* [Video file]. Retrieved from https://www.youtube.com/watch?v=wHYKBnI-Kfw

ReShel, A. (2016, July). *Healing Your Creativity after Trauma.* Retrieved from http://upliftconnect.com/healing-creativity

Rodrigues, V. & Friedman, H. L. (2015). Transpersonal Psychotherapies. In H. L. Friedman & G. Hartelius (Eds.), *The Wiley-Blackwell Handbook of Transpersonal Psychology*. West Sussex: John Wiley and Sons.

Rowan, J. (1993/1999). *The Transpersonal*. Hove: Brunner-Routledge.

Rowan, J. (2001). *Ordinary Ecstasy: The Dialectics of Humanistic Psychology*. Oxon: Routledge.

Sagan, C. (1980). *Cosmos*. New York: Random House.

Sartre, J. P. (1943). *Being and Nothingness.* New York: Phil. Library.

Scheflin, A. W., & Shapiro, J. L. (1989). *Trance on Trial*. New York: Guildford Press.

Scotton, B. W. (1996). Introduction and Definition of Transpersonal Psychiatry. In B.W. Scotton, A.B. Chinen & J. R. Battista(Eds.), *Textbook of Transpersonal Psychiatry and Psychology (pp. 2-8).* New York: Basic Books.

Shapiro, D. H. (2017). *Meditation: Self-Regulation Strategy and Altered State of Consciousness*. New York: Routledge.

Shroder, T. (1999). *Old Souls: Compelling Evidence from Children Who Remember Past Lives.* New York: Simon & Schuster.

Sion, A. (2010). *The Logic of Causation: Definition, Induction and Deduction of Deterministic Causality*. Geneva: Avi Sion.

Soul. (2017). In *Collins English Dictionary*. Retrieved from https://www.collinsdictionary.com/dictionary/english/soul

Stevenson, I. (1994). A Case of the Psychotherapist's Fallacy: Hypnotic Regression to "Previous Lives". *American Journal of Clinical Hypnosis, 36*(3), 188–193.

Stevenson, I. (1995). *Twenty Cases Suggestive of Reincarnation*. Charlottesville: University Press of Virginia.

Stevenson, I. (2000). The Phenomenon of Claimed Memories of Previous Lives: Possible Interpretations and Importance. *Medical Hypotheses, 54*(4), 652–659.

Stuckey, H. L., & Nobel, J. (2010). The Connection between Art, Healing, and Public Health: A Review of Current Literature. *American Journal of Public Health, 100*(2), 254–263.

Taylor, K. (1994). *The Breathwork Experience: Exploration and Healing in Nonordinary States of Consciousness*. Santa Cruz: Hanford Mead Publishers.

Taylor, S. A. (2016). *The Akashic Records: Unlock the Infinite Power, Wisdom and Energy of the Universe*. London: Hay House.

Tomlinson, A. (2006). *Healing the Eternal Soul*. Hampshire: O Books.

Valandrey, C. (2014). *L'Amour dans le Sang (Love in the Blood)*. Paris: Le Cherche Midi.

Van der Kolk, B. (2015). *The Body Keeps the Score: Mind, Brain and Body in the Transformation of Trauma*. London: Penguin Books.

Van Deurzen-Smith, E. (1997). *Everyday Mysteries*. Hove: Brunner Routledge.

Van Praagh, J. (2017). *Wisdom From Your Spirit Guides*. Carlsbad, CA: Hay House, Inc.

Vitaterna, M. H., King, D. P., Chang, A. M., Kornhauser, J. M., Lowrey, P. L., McDonald, J. D., … Takahashi, J. S. (1994). Mutagenesis and Mapping of a Mouse Gene, Clock, Essential for Circadian Behavior. *Science (New York, N.Y.), 264*(5159), 719–725.

Walsh, R. (1995). The Problem of Suffering. *The Humanistic Psychologist, 23*(3), 345–357.

Walsh, R., & Vaughan, F. (1993). On Transpersonal Definitions. *Journal of Transpersonal Psychology, 25*(2), 125–182.

Weiss, B. (1995). *Through Time into Healing: How Past Life Regression Therapy Can Heal Mind, Body and Soul.* London: Piatkus.

Wilber, K. (2000). *Integral Psychology: Consciousness, Spirit, Psychology, Therapy*. Boston: Shambhala Publications.

Woolger, R. (1988). *Other Lives, Other Selves*. New York: Bantam Books.

Woolger, R. (2010). *Healing Your Past Lives: Exploring the Many Lives of the Soul*. Boulder: Sounds True, Inc.

Yehuda, R., Daskalakis, N. P., Bierer, L. M., Bader, H. N., Klenger, T., Holsboer, F., & Binder, E. B. (2016). Holocaust Exposure Induced Intergenerational Effects on FKBP5 Methylation. *Biological Psychiatry, 8*(5), 372–380.

Yusim, A. (2017). *Fulfilled: How the Science of Spirituality Can Help You Live a Happier, More Meaningful Life*. New York, Grand Central Publishing.

INDEX

A

B

C

D

E

I

J

K

L

M

N

O

P

Q

R

U

V

W

Z

Printed in Great Britain
by Amazon